30-Minute

Vegetarian
Mexican

Cookbook

Other titles in this series:

30-Minute Vegetarian Indian Cookbook

30-Minute Vegetarian Thai Cookbook (Fall/Winter 1998–99)

30-Minute

Vegetarian
Mexican

Cookbook

Sarah Beattie

THE ECCO PRESS

THE ECCO PRESS
100 West Broad Street
Hopewell, New Jersey 08525

Printed in the United States of America

Library of Congress Cataloging-in-Publication Data

Beattie, Sarah.
30-minute vegetarian Mexican cookbook / Sarah Beattie. — 1st Ecco ed.
p.   cm.
Includes index.
ISBN 0-88001-598-5
1. Vegetarian cookery.   2. Cookery, Mexican.   3. Quick and easy
cookery.   I. Title.
TX837.B375   1998
641.5'636'0972—dc21   97-51581
CIP

Designed by Typeworks
The text of this book is set in Spectrum
9 8 7 6 5 4 3 2 1
FIRST EDITION 1998

Contents

Acknowledgments

Thanks are due to: Donna Sclater; Sue Sharpe; Roz Denny, Tony at Sky Co., Tom at Rio Pacific and Dougie Bell's Lupe Pinto on the Great Nopalito Hunt; Pickering Library; *Lonely Planet & Rough Guide to Mexico*; Rick and Deann Bayless' *Authentic Mexican Cooking*—an invaluable reference book; Alan Balfour for apple juice; Wendy Coslett who is not responsible for any errors in my Spanish; Wanda Whiteley and most particularly to Clarissa Hyman.

Love and grateful thanks to Magdalena Gray, Dylan Beattie and especially Michael Gray for services above and beyond.

Introduction

Mexican food has long been popular in the United States, especially in Texas and the Southwest. It is now finding fans across the rest of the world.

Some of the traditional recipes take hours, if not days, to prepare. In this book shortcuts using modern kitchen slaves (the food processor, mixer and blender) have been found while avoiding the sacrifice of flavor. Influences from all over Mexico's diverse regions and from TexMex and CalMex have shaped the recipes.

The ancient Maya people called themselves the Children of the Corn. In many ways present-day Mexicans continue to be children of the corn. Corn is in tortillas, tamales, as vegetables, in soups, stews, drinks and puddings. But Mexicans are skilled at making this basic foodstuff interesting. From crisp and crunchy to soft and light, corn is deliciously versatile.

Chilies in dried and fresh guises wake up the flavors of Mexico: some are brightly fiery, some are sweetly mellow. Sharper notes are brought in with limes and tomatillos (little green tomatoes). The unctuousness of smooth avocados and thick sour cream tempers the heat. Flavorsome tomatoes add body to sauces. Beans are the backbone of many meals, with fresh cheeses and herbs to supplement them. Chocolate, once the food of the gods in Ancient Mexico, is found in rich savory sauces and warming drinks, with spices lifting them far beyond childhood's hot cocoa.

Mexican food is just right in the depths of a dreary winter but is equally at home in the garden on a balmy summer evening. It is great party food, picnic fare and for barbecues. The main ingredients are cheap, the preparation is often simple and it makes wholesome, filling family meals.

Stocking Up—Mexican Ingredients
If you are going to cook Mexican food, there are some ingredients you will have to find. What follows is a simple list with some sug-

gested alternatives, in case items are unavailable. Specialty mail-order suppliers are listed where appropriate for the few obscure items you may have difficulty in tracking down.

AVOCADOS

Mexicans eat more avocados per head of population than any other nation. Buy under-ripe and allow them to ripen in the fruit bowl. Avoid chilling as this deadens the flavor. Mexican Hass avocados are more appropriate than the Israeli Nabal and Fuerte varieties. An avocado is ready when the flesh gives under gentle pressure. In the Hass variety the skin turns from green to black.

CHEESE

Mexican cheeses, particularly the fresh ones, are available in some specialty cheese shops. Appropriate substitutions have been suggested throughout the book if authentic Mexican cheese is unavailable.

CHILIES

It would be possible to write a book just on Mexican chilies—there are hundreds of different chilies; they are available fresh, canned or dried, and they can have different names depending on the state they are in. But don't panic—here is a short guide. It is by no means comprehensive but will suffice as an introduction. When you have become addicted to the chilies, you can find out more. Please keep in mind, when you are seeding hot chilies wear rubber gloves!

Fresh

Habanero—squat, bright yellowish orange chili, very hot when ripe. Similar to the Jamaican scotch bonnet, which can be used instead.

Jalapeño—moderate to hot, bullet-shaped, usually green but sometimes red.

Poblano—a snub-nosed, large green chili, only moderately hot with a rich flavor. If unavailable, use kenyan or Anaheim.

Serrano—small, thin mostly green. Quite hot. Use small plain green chilies if unavailable.

Dried

Ancho—this is a dried poblano, all wrinkly and dark reddish-brown. Not very hot and quite fruity.

Chipotle—smoked jalapeños, with a fiery earthy flavor.

Guajillo—moderate, with an almost apricot tang—some describe it as "green tea" flavor.

Mulato—apart from being darker, this chili looks very similar to the ancho. It is full-flavored, a little smoky and moderately hot.

New Mexico Red—large mild chili, fairly sweet.

Pasado—a roasted dried chili with fruity flavors.

Pasilla—sometimes sold as negro due to its blackish skin. Moderately hot with a taste of Pomfret cakes and raisins. A slightly smoky scent.

Note

Several of these dried chilies are available in powdered form—this can save considerable cooking time, and it is a useful way of adding extra flavor quickly. Many of these fresh and dried chilies are available at Hispanic markets and by mail order from Kitchen, New York, NY, tel. (212) 243-4433. If you have a Mexican restaurant nearby, ask them who their suppliers are.

Canned

Chipotle—a smoked jalapeño.

Green—unnamed green chilies are available, peeled and canned.

Serrano—available pickled.

CHOCOLATE

Ibarra Mexican cooking chocolate can be found through specialty shops and by mail order from Kitchen, New York, NY, tel. (212) 243-4433. It contains sugar, cinnamon and almonds. If you cannot find it, use a good dark chocolate with some cinnamon as directed in the recipes.

CORN

Corn is the most commonly used cereal in Mexican cooking. For speed, instant polenta (Italian part-cooked cornmeal) is used in some recipes. If this is not specified, then regular, medium-ground cornmeal (maize meal) is to be used. Do not confuse cornmeal with cornstarch—the fine white thickening agent. Corn on the cob is also used, but to save time canned or frozen kernels can be substituted. Ready-made corn tortillas are available in various forms. Try the different sorts and find a brand you like. If you are going to make your own regularly, you will need to invest in a tortilla press—see good kitchen equipment specialists and department stores. Corn tortillas are made with *masa harina*—a treated cornmeal, which has been "limed" (lime is added to increase the nutritional value of the cornmeal), soaked, ground with water and then dried and powdered. In the United States *masa harina* is available in supermarkets under the Quaker brand and by mail order from Maria and Ricardo's Tortilla Factory, Jamaica Plain, MA, tel. (617) 524-6107.

FLOUR TORTILLAS

Long shelf-life wheat flour tortillas are sold in many supermarkets. It is well worth keeping a couple of packets in the larder for quick meals.

HERBS

Mexicans use *epazote*, also known as pigweed or wormseed. It is difficult to find, so I have not included it in any of the recipes in this book. It has a rather rank, bitter, pungent flavor. I suspect that it is used mainly for its medicinal properties—it is a vermifuge, ridding the body of intestinal worms! Other herbs are used as flavorsome alternatives. Coriander (cilantro) is also widely used in Mexican cooking, and it is well worth cultivating even if you only have room for a pot on the windowsill. Marjoram or oregano and parsley are also used.

NOPALES OR NOPALITOS

These are cactus stems. Although they are available fresh in the United States, to use fresh cactus requires very time-consuming preparation, which would put it out of the scope of this book. Commercially prepared cactus salsa is available.

OIL

Except where otherwise specified, use a good corn or vegetable oil.

RICE

Carolina or Java rice—the shorter of the long grains—are the closest to Mexican rice that are widely available.

SOUR CREAM

Mexican sour cream is thicker than the dairy product available in the United States—use crème fraîche for a more authentic texture and flavor.

SUGAR

Traditional Mexican cooks use an unrefined sugar that comes in hard cones—much like the palm sugar or jaggery of Southeast Asia. As this is not readily available, light brown sugar has been substituted.

TOMATILLOS

Small green "tomatoes" in papery husks like physalis (Cape Gooseberries). Available fresh in the United States from specialty food shops, such as Kitchen, New York, NY, tel. (212) 243-4433, you are more likely to be able to find them canned. They are not the same as under-ripe tomatoes; *but,* if you have some unripe cherry tomatoes, you can use them, provided you salt them first to draw out any bitterness. If the tomatillos are added to a sauce for piquancy, substitute chopped gherkins or capers for a similar flavor.

TOMATOES

Flavorsome tomatoes, especially the plum and Marmande varieties, should be used when fresh are called for. Canned whole or crushed tomatoes are often used for speed.

30-Minute

Vegetarian Mexican

Cookbook

Basic Recipes

Corn Tortillas

Makes 12 tortillas

Corn tortillas are more widely used in Mexico; the wheat flour ones are normally only found in the north. However, they are much more difficult to make at home as you require *masa harina*, a cornmeal flour that has been specially prepared by soaking it in lime water, and to make life a little easier, a tortilla press. Canned, uncooked tortillas are available as are pre-cooked ones that require reheating. If, however, you fancy a spot of do-it-yourself, here is the recipe. Two people will make much faster work of this; build up a rhythm—one to press and one to cook—and it can be done in 20 minutes.

1½ cups *masa harina*
1 cup warm water
a good pinch of salt

24 squares of wax paper approx.
8 inches

1) Place all the ingredients in a food processor with the kneading attachment and process for 3–5 minutes.
2) Cover the base of the tortilla press with a square of wax paper.
3) Pinch off a piece of dough the size of a walnut and put it on the paper. Cover with a second sheet of wax paper and close the press.
4) Open and peel off the top sheet of paper. If it sticks, the dough is too wet; return to the processor with a little more *masa harina*. If the edges are cracked and crumbly, the dough is too dry; return to the processor with 1 teaspoon of water. If it comes away from the paper and the edges are smooth, form the rest of the tortillas in the same way between two sheets of paper.

5) Invert a tortilla onto a moderately hot griddle or heavy frying pan. Peel off the paper backing. Cook for 1–2 minutes on each side until lightly speckled brown.

6) Remove and place on a clean dish towel where it will soften as it cools. For crisp tortillas or tacos, fry before serving.

Flour Tortillas

Makes 16—24 tortillas

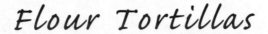

Flour tortillas are available ready-made in most supermarkets. They have a shelf life of several months, or they can be frozen. It is always worth keeping a few packets in your store cupboard.

It isn't very time consuming to make your own though, and it is very satisfying. Using a food processor means there's no donkey work, and you can double the quantities to stock the freezer with homemade tortillas.

4½ cups plain flour
1—2 teaspoons salt

3 oz. vegetable shortening or
   margarine, cut into small
   pieces
boiling water

1) Place the flour and salt in the food processor with the kneading attachment and mix.
2) Put the fat into a heatproof measuring cup. Add the boiling water up to the 1 cup mark. Stir to melt the fat.
3) Pour into the food processor on low speed. Continue processing for 3 minutes, as the dough forms into a soft ball.
4) Divide into 24 or 16 pieces or just pinch off walnut-sized pieces of dough as you need them. Keep the rest of the dough covered (the processor bowl with the lid on is ideal). Roll out the balls of dough very thinly.

5) Place on a moderately hot ungreased griddle or heavy skillet. Cook for 1 minute on the first side and 30 seconds on the other.

6) Pile onto foil or wax paper as they are cooked; then reheat, loosely wrapped, for 2–3 minutes in a moderate oven.

7) You can freeze them, interleaved with wax paper and wrapped, or in an air-tight plastic storage container. To cook from frozen, place on the griddle for 30 seconds each side.

Quick Tamales

Serves 4–6

*T*amale purists will probably throw up their hands in horror—tamale making is normally such a long-winded affair. However, these tasty torpedoes of cornmeal flecked with chili are tender from steaming, are really good with just-melted butter and can be made in under 30 minutes.

Strictly speaking, tamales are steamed, wrapped in corn husks or banana leaves. As these two items are not easily available, have ready 12 squares of wax paper.

Salsa or moles can be used to accompany them. A Sweet Tamales recipe can be found on page 126.

1⅓ cups vegetable stock or
   water
1 cup instant polenta
1–2 teaspoons coarsely ground
   red chili

½ teaspoon salt
1 tablespoon butter or
   margarine
2 teaspoons baking powder

1) Mix all the ingredients together in a saucepan and cook over moderate heat until the mixture is thick and leaves the sides of the pan. Beat well.

2) Divide between 12 sheets of wax paper, shape like cigars and roll up loosely. Twist the ends of the papers and steam in a covered pan for 20 minutes. Serve.

Refried Beans (Frijoles Refritos)

2 cups canned pinto or black-eyed beans, drained and rinsed

3–4 tablespoons vegetable oil

Serves 4–6

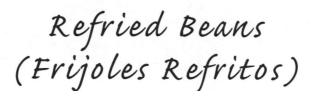

1) In a heavy skillet fry the beans in the oil over moderately high heat. Stir around with the back of a wooden spoon, pressing the beans together to form a cake. When a crust forms on the base, turn over and fry the other side. Serve.

Soup

Sopa de Fideos

Serves 4–6

Noodle soup, Mexican style. Less soupy than one might imagine, this is quite a substantial dish.

2 cups egg noodles	salt and pepper
oil for deep-frying	pinch of brown sugar
2 onions, finely chopped	1 teaspoon dried marjoram or
2 cloves garlic, crushed	oregano
1–2 serrano chilies, seeded and finely chopped	
1 small green pepper, seeded and chopped	*To Finish*
	chopped coriander (cilantro)
1 cup crushed tomatoes	grated dry cheese such as
2 cups vegetable stock	Spanish mahon or a grana, e.g., parmesan

1) In a large, deep skillet fry the noodles in the oil very briefly. Drain and set aside.
2) Pour off all but a couple of tablespoons of oil. Add the onions, garlic, chilies and pepper. Sauté for a couple of minutes and add the noodles, tomatoes, and stock. Season to taste with salt and pepper.
3) Add the sugar and herbs. Simmer for 20 minutes, stirring from time to time.
4) Serve garnished with the coriander (cilantro) and cheese. Alternatively, serve topped with a good dollop of sour cream and a sprinkle of broken corn chips in each bowl.

Sopa de Arroz Rojos

Serves 4–6

Red rice "soup," as opposed to the next recipe for green rice "soup"! This is another of those "dry soups" that are eaten as a first course. They are so filling that served with some cheese and a salad, I think they are a meal in themselves.

2 tablespoons oil
1 cup uncooked rice
1 small onion, chopped
2 cloves garlic, crushed
1 pasado chili, crumbled
½ teaspoon ground cumin

1½ cups crushed tomatoes
½ cup water
½ cup canned sweet corn
1 red bell pepper, diced
salt and pepper

1) In a saucepan heat the oil over moderately high heat. Add the rice, and cook, stirring for 2 minutes.

2) Add the onion, garlic, chili and cumin. Stir over moderate heat for a couple of minutes.

3) Add the tomatoes and water. Cover and cook for 10 minutes on a low heat. Add the sweet corn and bell pepper and cook for 5 minutes more. Season and serve.

Arroz Verde

Serves 4–6

Keeping the green theme, if you can find fresh tomatillos complete with their husks, use them to decorate this one-dish meal. Otherwise an extra sprinkle of coriander (cilantro) and some lime wedges will do.

2 tablespoons oil
1 cup uncooked rice
2 cloves garlic, crushed
a bunch of spring onions (scallions), chopped—including the green sections
1–2 serrano chilies, seeded and chopped

½ teaspoon ground cumin
2 cups vegetable stock
2 tablespoons chopped flat parsley
2 tablespoons chopped coriander (cilantro)
½ cup peas—fresh or frozen
salt and pepper

1) In a saucepan heat the oil over moderately high heat and in it cook the rice over moderate heat for 2–3 minutes.

2) Add the garlic, spring onions (scallions), chilies and cumin. Cook for 2–3 minutes then add the stock and the herbs.

3) Bring to a boil and simmer for 10 minutes. Add the peas. Cook for a further 3 minutes, season and serve.

Corn Soup

Serves 4—6

1 onion, chopped

2 tablespoons oil

2 canned chipotle chilies, sliced

two 10 oz.cans creamed sweet
   corn

water

1 bay leaf

salt and pepper

1) In a saucepan cook the onion in the oil over moderate heat, until golden. Add the chilies and cook for 1 minute.

2) Stir in the sweet corn and enough water to give the consistency of half-and-half.

3) Add the bay leaf and season well with salt and pepper. Simmer for 10 minutes. Serve.

Sopa de Almendrada Verde

Serves 4–6

*H*ave this soup hot or well chilled.

2 cups potatoes, cubed
1 cup blanched almonds
2 green serrano chilies, seeded
4 tablespoons flat-leafed
   parsley

1 clove garlic, crushed
water
ice cubes (optional)

1) In a large saucepan boil the potatoes in salted water until tender.

2) Pour 1 cup of the water from the potatoes over the almonds in a blender. Blend until smooth. Scrape into a sieve and squeeze out as much liquid as possible.

3) Return this almond "milk" to the cleaned out blender with the potato, chilies, parsley, garlic and 2 cups of cold water. Blend until well combined and then strain through a fine sieve.

4) Season very well. Serve with an ice cube or two in prechilled bowls or reheat slowly, making sure not to boil.

Gazpacho

Serves 4–6

*T*here are many Spanish dishes that Mexicans have made their own. Gazpacho is one of them. Avocado and chili are not found in most Old World recipes. This is a quick version. As with most chilled soups, it would benefit from longer standing time to allow the flavors to develop. Ensure that all ingredients are chilled before you start and season well; then the speed won't matter too much.

This dish is quite substantial. Serve followed by some nachos or tostadas and most will be more than satisfied.

3 cups crushed tomatoes

2 crushed cloves garlic

4 spring onions (scallions), chopped

2 serrano chilies, seeded and finely shredded

½ a cucumber, peeled and chopped

juice of a lime

2 tablespoons olive oil

3 tablespoons bread crumbs or crushed tortillas

2 tablespoons chopped coriander (cilantro)

1 teaspoon cumin

1 ripe avocado, peeled and diced

1) Purée everything, except the avocado, in a blender in bursts until well mixed. Stir in the avocado and season to taste. Thin if necessary with a little ice-cold water.

2) You can serve with little bowls of chopped hard-boiled eggs, olives, croutons, capers, etc. for diners to add as desired.

Sopa de Lima

Serves 4–6

The best vegetable stock comes from celeriac and other aromatic roots such as carrots. Save the water when boiling these vegetables and freeze in ice cube trays. However, good fresh stocks are now available in supermarkets or, in a pinch, use vegetable bouillon cubes.

2 tablespoons oil
1 onion, quartered
2 cloves garlic
1 tablespoon tomato paste
1 teaspoon Caribe powdered
   chili or New Mexico Red, if
   Caribe is unavailable

5 cups vegetable stock
juice of 1½ limes
sour cream (optional)
coriander (cilantro) (optional)

1) Using a food processor, process the oil, onion and garlic to a paste. Scrape into a large heavy saucepan and cook until nicely browned.

2) Add the tomato paste and powdered chili and cook, stirring until the mixture darkens.

3) Add the stock and simmer for 15 minutes. Add the lime juice. Season to taste and serve with a swirl of sour cream and a sprig of coriander (cilantro).

Sopa de Nopalitos

Serves 4–6

*C*actus soup sounds a little odd, but it is quite delicious.

4 onions, chopped
2 cloves garlic, chopped
1 jalapeño, chopped
1 tablespoon oil
12 oz. cactus pieces, drained,
   rinsed and cubed

4 cups vegetable stock
½ teaspoon dried oregano
a pinch of dried rosemary
salt and pepper
1 egg, lightly beaten
2 teaspoons lime juice

1) In a large saucepan cook the onions, garlic and jalapeño in oil until softened. Add the cactus pieces and fry another 2 minutes. Add the stock and the herbs and season well. Simmer 15 minutes.

2) Put the egg and lime juice in a soup tureen. Add the soup by the ladleful, stirring continuously. Serve. If you need to reheat, do not boil.

Sopa Tascara

Serves 4–6

A creamy bean soup—this reminds me of Indian dhal, a roasted chili taking the place of the fried garlic.

2 teaspoons oil
2 onions, roughly chopped
2 serrano chilies
2 cloves garlic
2 carrots, chopped
1 stick celery, chopped
1 bay leaf
2 cloves
4 cups water
salt and pepper

14 oz. can pinto beans, rinsed
and drained
6 tablespoons crème fraîche
(available at specialty food
shops and some supermar-
kets)
1 cup grated cheese—mild
cheddar or Monterey Jack
2 guajillo chilies, fried and
chopped

1) In a saucepan cook the onions and serrano chilies for 3 minutes until brown. Add the garlic, carrot, celery, bay leaf and cloves. Cook, stirring, for another minute. Add the water and season well with salt and pepper. Boil for 15 minutes.

2) Purée the beans. Strain the water onto the beans. Simmer, stirring occasionally, for 5 minutes. Check seasoning. Serve with a spoon of crème fraîche stirred through each bowl and a sprinkle of cheese and guajillo added at the last moment.

Sopa de Garbanzos

Serves 4–6

Not "garbage soup" as my daughter misheard. "Garbanzo" is the Spanish name for chick pea. Epazote is the usual herb for this hearty soup, but since it is hard to find, I suggest using rosemary.

16 small strong onions, peeled and quartered—pickling onions are ideal

3 cloves garlic, chopped

3 carrots, scraped and diced

1 leek, sliced

1 tablespoon oil

4 cups vegetable stock or water

14 oz. can chick peas

a large sprig of rosemary

a bay leaf

pepper

salt

1 chipotle chili, fried and sliced

¾ cup crumbled feta cheese

1) In a large saucepan cook the onions, garlic, carrots and leek in the oil until browned.

2) Add the stock or water, chick peas, rosemary and bay leaf. Season with pepper. Simmer for 20 minutes. Season with salt.

3) Serve with the addition of a sprinkle of chipotle and a spoon of cheese in each bowl.

Tortilla Soup

Serves 4–6

*I*f you have time you can fry your own tortilla strips, but packaged ones make quite a good substitute. Freeze-dried chilies can also be used instead of frying your own, but here there is a real difference in flavor.

1 onion, chopped
2 cloves garlic, crushed
2 cups crushed tomatoes
oil
4 cups vegetable stock
2 tablespoons chopped
   coriander (cilantro)

2 tablespoons chopped mint
4 dried ancho or pasilla chilies
½ cup cheddar or Monterey
   Jack cheese, diced
6 oz. crumbled white tortilla
   chips

1) In a large saucepan cook the onion, garlic and tomatoes in 3 tablespoons of oil over moderate heat, stirring, for 5 minutes. Add the stock and chopped herbs. Season well and simmer.

2) Meanwhile, in a small skillet fry the chilies in some heated oil until crisp—this will only take about half a minute. Drain and crumble.

3) Serve the soup and allow diners to sprinkle with the cheese, chilies and tortilla strips.

Salsas and Moles

Chiltomate

Serves 4–6

Avery fiery, smooth tomato sauce from the Yucatán region. Traditionally, it calls for epazote—pigweed or wormseed—but as that is very difficult for most cooks to find, I have omitted it and used a sprig of rosemary instead.

2 habanero chilies, seeded
1 small onion
1 clove garlic
14 oz can chopped tomatoes
1 tablespoon oil

the juice of 1 Seville orange—if
   unavailable use ½ an orange
   and ½ a lime
1 sprig rosemary
salt and pepper

1) Purée the chilies, onion, garlic and tomatoes until smooth in a food processor.
2) In a heavy skillet fry the purée in the hot oil, stirring, for 5 minutes.
3) Add the orange juice, rosemary and a good pinch of salt and pepper.
4) Simmer on low heat for another 5 minutes. Discard the rosemary and serve.

Guacamole

Serves 4–6

Guacamole is an avocado dip. In true Mexican cooking the avocado tends to be chopped rather than puréed. In TexMex it is sometimes mixed with sour cream. Although this may not be entirely authentic, it is delicious. There are many different ways to make Guacamole, so I have included three versions.

1 small onion, very finely
  chopped
1–2 serrano chilies, finely
  chopped
2 large ripe avocados, peeled
  and roughly chopped

1 good pinch of salt
juice of ½ a lime
1 large tomato, peeled, seeded
  and diced
2 tablespoons chopped
  coriander (cilantro)

1) Place the onion, chilies and avocados together in a bowl and mash with a fork. Mix in the salt, lime juice, tomato and coriander (cilantro), stirring well. Serve with tortilla chips or crudités.

Guacamole II

Serves 4–6

2 large avocados
2 cloves garlic, crushed
juice of ½ a lime

salt and pepper
cayenne pepper
4 oz. sour cream (optional)

1) Purée the avocados, garlic and lime juice in a food processor or blender until smooth. Season to taste with salt, pepper and cayenne pepper.

2) Fold through the sour cream—if using. If you don't combine thoroughly you will be left with a marbled effect which is quite pretty.

Guacamole III

Serves 4–6

*T*his guacamole is more in the vein of the Californian inspired salsa. Use it as a dip or as a salad dressing.

1 small onion, finely chopped
2 cloves garlic, crushed
1–2 serrano chilies, finely chopped
2 large avocados, peeled and diced
1 large tomato, peeled, seeded and diced

juice of ½ a lime
2 tablespoons chopped coriander (cilantro)
olive oil
salt and pepper

1) In a bowl mix together the onion, garlic, chilies, avocados, tomato, lime juice and coriander (cilantro). Add enough oil to give it a runny consistency. Season with salt and pepper and serve.

Mole Oaxaqueño

Serves 4–6

This sauce from the Oaxaca region sounds rather curious, but try it over Tamales (see page 7).

1 medium onion, chopped

2 cloves garlic, chopped

1 small bulb fennel, chopped

1 medium banana, diced

2 tablespoons oil plus extra if required

2 tablespoons sesame seeds

2 tablespoons raisins

2 tablespoons ground almonds

2 tablespoons bread crumbs

1¾ cups crushed tomatoes

½ teaspoon ground bay leaf

a good grinding of black pepper

2 teaspoons ground cinnamon

1 teaspoon oregano

1 oz dark chocolate, grated

4 ancho chilies, soaked and puréed

1 tablespoon natural peanut butter

½ cup water

1) In a saucepan cook the onion, garlic, fennel and banana in the oil over moderate heat until softened. Remove with a slotted spoon and transfer to a food processor.

2) Add the sesame seeds, raisins, almonds and bread crumbs to the pan and cook gently until the mixture begins to color.

3) Add to the food processor with the tomatoes, bay leaf, pepper, cinnamon, oregano and chocolate. Process until fairly smooth.

4) In a saucepan fry the chili purée over moderate heat, adding a little more oil if required.

5) Stir in the contents of the food processor and add the peanut butter. Cook, stirring, for 2 minutes and then add the water. Simmer for 10 minutes. Serve.

Mole Pepitas

Serves 4–6

Spoon this smooth pumpkin seed sauce over grilled vegetables, or use it in the Yucatan specialty, Papadzules (see page 61).

2 tablespoons oil	a generous grinding of black
1 small onion, chopped	pepper
2 cloves garlic, crushed	a good pinch of salt
1 tablespoon powdered ancho	1 pinch of ground allspice
chilies	a pinch of ground cloves
½ cup toasted pumpkin seeds,	1 teaspoon brown sugar
finely ground	1 teaspoon cinnamon
1 tablespoon natural peanut	a pinch of dried oregano
butter	3 cups vegetable stock
2 tablespoons bread crumbs	1 tablespoon butter

1) In a skillet over moderate heat, cook the onion and garlic in the oil until soft and brown. Add the powdered chili and cook, stirring, for 1 minute.

2) Place in a blender with the pumpkin seeds, peanut butter, bread crumbs and seasonings. Add only as much stock as is needed to process the mixture smoothly.

3) Scrape out the mixture and return to the skillet. Cook the mixture in the butter for 4 minutes, stirring constantly. Stir in the remaining stock and simmer for another 10 minutes.

Mole Poblano

Serves 4—6

Mole Poblano is a chili sauce often enriched with chocolate. Usually meats are served in it. It can be used very simply over roasted vegetables or cornbread pudding. The choice of chocolate is very important. Most commercial brands are very sweet. Find a very dark plain one with at least 65% cocoa solids. There are specialty Mexican cooking chocolates available (see page xi).

The ingredients' list may seem a little daunting, but don't be put off; the method is simple and it won't take that long.

3 tablespoons sesame seeds
½ cup ground almonds
½ cup raisins
1 teaspoon ground cinnamon
½ teaspoon ground cumin
½ teaspoon ground coriander
　(cilantro)
¼ teaspoon ground black
　pepper
½ teaspoon ground aniseed or
　fennel seeds
4 mulato chilies, soaked, torn
　into pieces
4 pasilla chilies, soaked, torn
　into pieces

4 ancho chilies, soaked, torn
　into pieces
2 fresh red cayenne chilies,
　chopped
1 large onion, roughly chopped
3 cloves garlic, crushed
8 oz. can chopped or crushed
　tomatoes
1 cup bread crumbs
2 tablespoons oil
2 cups vegetable stock
1 oz dark chocolate

1) Toast the sesame seeds in a dry skillet over moderate heat. When just browned, stir in the almonds, raisins and spices. Stir for 30 seconds then scrape into a blender or food processor.

2) Add the chilies, onion, garlic, tomatoes and bread crumbs. Process to a fairly smooth paste. If it is too heavy, add a tablespoon or two of the stock—no more, though or it will be too sloppy.

3) Heat the oil in the skillet over low heat and fry the chili paste for 5 minutes. Add the stock slowly. Then stir in the chocolate. Cook slowly for 15 minutes.

Mango Salsa

Serves 4–6

*P*art of the new wave sweeping the Mexican resorts, mango salsa combines new ideas with traditional methods. Fruity and fragrant, it adds a fresh note to Burritos or Quesadillas (see pages 40 and 86).

2 just-ripe mangoes, peeled and diced

1 small onion, chopped

1 serrano chili, finely chopped

2 tablespoons coriander (cilantro), chopped

juice of ½ a lime

¼ teaspoon salt

a pinch of brown sugar

a generous grinding of black pepper

1) In a bowl mix everything together and serve.

Cook's Note

Green (under-ripe) mangoes can be used for a very tangy, crunchy salsa, but omit the lime juice and add a little more sugar.

Pepper Salsa

Serves 4–6

To roast the peppers, either char them over an open flame or on a rack set over an electric burner, turning until blackened, about 5 minutes. When the skin has blackened and become papery, it is very easy to remove. Wait until peppers are cool enough to handle before peeling.

2 jalapeño chilies, roasted,
  peeled and finely chopped
1 small red bell pepper, roasted,
  peeled and thinly sliced
1 small red onion, chopped

juice of a lime
2 cloves garlic, crushed
a good pinch of salt
a small bunch of fresh coriander (cilantro), chopped

1) In a bowl simply mix all the ingredients together. Allow to stand for 20 minutes before serving.

Quick Adobo

Makes 1 small jar

᠅

*U*se this sauce as a marinade—smear it on vegetables before grilling, broiling or frying—or use a spoonful to perk up a soup or casserole.

2 teaspoons garlic purée
1 tablespoon tomato purée
2 tablespoons vinegar—cider
   or white wine vinegar
1–2 teaspoons ancho chili
   powder
1 teaspoon New Mexico Red
   chili powder

pinch of ground cloves
pinch of ground cumin
½ teaspoon ground cinnamon
¼ teaspoon ground bay leaf
1 teaspoon salt
a generous amount of freshly
   ground black pepper

1) In a bowl simply mix all the ingredients together well. Store in a clean jar in the refrigerator.

Quick Red Onion Preserve

Makes 1 jar

Red onion marmalades and preserves have been snatched up by New Wave cooks, but they aren't new. Mexicans have been eating them for years. They are delicious with simple egg dishes or cheese.

3 red onions, peeled and sliced	½ teaspoon crushed black
2 cloves garlic, sliced	peppercorns
a scant ½ cup cider vinegar or	½ teaspoon salt
white wine vinegar	¼ teaspoon ground cumin
1 tablespoon water	2 tablespoons superfine sugar

1) Put everything except the cumin and sugar into a pan and bring to a boil. Simmer for 5 minutes.
2) Add the cumin and the sugar, stir to dissolve and then boil hard until thickened.
3) Jar and store in a cool place or use immediately.

Cook's Note

Lime juice can be used instead of vinegar—use the juice of 1 lime topped off with water to make a scant ½ cup.

Salsa Cruda

Serves 4–6

Raw sauce! This is one of the simplest sauces you can make, and you'll find yourself using it for all sorts of dishes, not just with Mexican food. Freshness is all. You can use a food processor to chop everything, but have a light hand on the pulse button—you don't want a purée.

4 medium tomatoes—seeded, peeled and chopped	2 tablespoons chopped coriander (cilantro)
2 spring onions (scallions), chopped	¼ teaspoon salt
2 serrano chilies, chopped	½ teaspoon sugar
	2 tablespoons oil (optional)

1) In a bowl mix everything together, using the oil if the salsa is to be used as a salad dressing.

Tomato Sauce

Serves 4–6

*T*his recipe has virtually the same ingredients as the previous salsa, but this one is cooked briefly before serving.

4 tomatoes, roughly chopped
4 spring onions (scallions),
　chopped
1–2 cloves garlic, crushed
2 serrano chilies, chopped
¼ teaspoon salt

½ teaspoon sugar
2 tablespoons oil
2 tablespoons chopped
　coriander (cilantro) or flat-
　leafed parsley

1) Put everything except the oil and coriander (cilantro), or parsley, into a food processor and process for a few seconds. In a skillet cook the paste in the oil over moderate heat until it thickens—about 5 minutes. Stir to avoid burning. Add the coriander (cilantro), or parsley, and serve.

Xnipec

Serves 4–6

X*nipec,* or "nose of the dog," is a very fiery sauce typical of the Yucatan region. Made with habanero or scotch bonnet chilies and the local bitter oranges known as *mamey,* this salsa is not for the fainthearted—you have been warned! Use this as a serious challenge to those swaggering braggarts we all know, the ones who demand the ultimate chili or the hottest vindaloo! If you cannot find Seville (bitter) oranges, use a blend of sweet orange juice with lemon or lime. If you prefer a less intimidating level of chili heat, use a milder chili.

2 yellow habanero chilies,
   finely chopped
2 small onions, finely chopped
1 large tomato, peeled, seeded
   and finely chopped

2 tablespoons Seville (bitter)
   orange juice or see above
salt to taste

1)   In a bowl simply mix everything together and serve.

Cook's Note

Adding sugar is not authentic, but it does temper the chilies' heat—but only slightly!

Main Courses

Burritos

Makes 8

*B*urritos are northern Mexican fare, using wheat flour as opposed to corn tortillas.

2 onions, roughly chopped

1 jalapeño chili, chopped

2 tablespoons oil

1 clove garlic, chopped

14 oz. can pinto beans, rinsed
and drained

3 tomatoes, chopped

2 tablespoons chopped
coriander (cilantro)

salt and pepper

8 wheat flour tortillas, warmed

3 cups grated münster or
gouda cheese

1) In a skillet cook the onions and chili in the oil until they begin to color.

2) Add the garlic and beans. Crush the beans slightly while cooking.

3) Add the tomatoes and coriander (cilantro). Cook, stirring, for 5 minutes. Season with salt and pepper.

4) Spread each tortilla with the bean mixture. Sprinkle thickly with cheese, roll up and serve immediately.

Baked Burritos

Makes 8

2 tablespoons oil
2 onions, chopped
1 jalapeño chili, chopped
2 cloves garlic, chopped
12 oz can flageolet beans
1 cup peas, fresh or frozen

⅔ cup sour cream
salt and pepper
8 flour tortillas
2½ cups grated münster or
　gouda cheese

1)　In a skillet cook the onion and chili until softened and add the garlic. Cook until they begin to color. Add the flageolet beans and peas. Stir and then add the sour cream. Season well.

2)　Divide between the tortillas and roll up. Put in a baking dish and sprinkle with cheese. Bake in a preheated 400°F oven for 10 minutes. Serve.

Black Beans in Beer

Serves 4–6

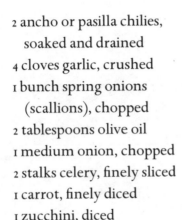

2 ancho or pasilla chilies,
  soaked and drained
4 cloves garlic, crushed
1 bunch spring onions
  (scallions), chopped
2 tablespoons olive oil
1 medium onion, chopped
2 stalks celery, finely sliced
1 carrot, finely diced
1 zucchini, diced

1 small red bell pepper, diced
1 small green bell pepper, diced
3 medium tomatoes, skinned
  and chopped
14 oz can black beans
½ bottle Mexican beer
4 crisp corn tortillas
1 cup cheddar or Monterey
  Jack cheese, grated

1) Put the chilies, garlic, spring onions (scallions) and oil into a blender and blend to a paste.

2) Scrape into a heavy skillet and cook for 1 minute over moderate heat. Add the onion, celery, carrot, zucchini and peppers. Cook for a couple of minutes, and then add the tomatoes and black beans. Cook for 1 minute; then add the beer. Season with salt and pepper.

3) Layer the bean mixture with the tortillas into an ovenproof dish. Sprinkle with the cheese and bake in a preheated 450°F oven for 10 minutes. Serve.

Chiles Rellenos

Makes 6

Stuffed chilies, dipped in batter and then deep-fried.

6 poblano chilies

1 onion, chopped

2 large mushrooms, chopped

2 tablespoons butter

½ teaspoon ground cumin

4 tablespoons cooked rice or
    bread crumbs

1 cup mozzarella, diced

salt and pepper

4 eggs, separated

2 tablespoons flour

oil for deep-frying

1) Roast the poblanos on a rack set over an electric burner, turning until the skins are blackened. When the peppers are cool enough to handle, peel, make a slit in the side and scrape out the seeds.

2) In a skillet cook the onion and mushrooms in the butter over moderate heat. When browned, add the cumin, rice or bread crumbs and cheese. Mix well and season. Remove the stuffing from the heat.

3) In a bowl whisk the egg whites until stiff. In another bowl beat the yolks until pale. Fold the yolks into the whites with the flour.

4) Fill the poblanos with the stuffing and then dip in the egg mixture.

5) In a heavy, deep skillet, heat about 3 inches oil over moderately high heat. Gently drop the poblanos into the hot oil and fry until crisp and golden. Serve immediately.

Cook's Note

The chilies can be filled with leftover Refried Beans (see page 7).

Black Bean Chili Verde

Serves 4–6

*T*his is a "green" chili. Serrano chilies are much hotter than Anaheim but Anaheim are much bigger—make your choice according to taste and the market.

3 green bell peppers
2 serrano or Anaheim chilies, seeded
1 bunch spring onions (scallions), chopped
5 tomatillos, if available
4 cups fresh spinach
4 cloves garlic, crushed
2 large cooking onions, roughly chopped

2 tablespoons vegetable oil
2 cups mushrooms
14 oz can black beans, rinsed and drained
1 tablespoon ground cumin
2 teaspoons brown sugar
2 tablespoons freshly chopped coriander (cilantro)

1) Roast the bell peppers and the chilies as instructed on page 97.
2) Remove the blackened skin and the seeds and place in a food processor with the spring onions (scallions), tomatillos and spinach. Process to make a purée.
3) In a large skillet sauté the garlic and onions in the oil over moderate heat, stirring, until browned. Add the mushrooms and cook until the juices run.
4) Add the beans and the pepper purée. Cook, stirring.
5) Add the cumin and sugar. Simmer for 10 minutes. Stir in the coriander (cilantro) and serve.

Chard or Spinach Empanadas

Makes 12

Empanadas are turnovers, akin to Indian samosas. In fact, the dough is very similar. Traditionally they are deep-fried, but in this version they are baked in a hot oven for speed.

It is a bit of a sprint to make a dozen empanadas in 30 minutes, but it is possible. An extra pair of hands when rolling and filling will speed you on your way.

Filling
1 small onion, chopped
2 cloves garlic
1 serrano chili, finely chopped
1 tablespoon oil, butter or
    vegetable margarine
2 tomatoes, chopped
4½ cups Swiss chard or spinach,
    washed, dried and cut or
    torn into strips

a good pinch of ground allspice
salt and pepper

oil

Dough
¾ cup boiling water
¼ cup soft butter or margarine
½ teaspoon salt
2½ cups flour

1) Preheat the oven to 450°F.
2) In a large skillet sauté the onion, garlic and chili in the oil over moderate heat, stirring, for a couple of minutes until softened.
3) Add the tomatoes and chard or spinach. Cook, stirring from time to time, until reduced and the liquid has been boiled off. Season with allspice, salt and pepper.

4) Put a couple of roasting pans in the oven with enough oil to cover the bottoms.

5) Place all the dough ingredients in a food processor with a dough attachment. Process until a soft dough is formed.

6) Divide the dough into 12 balls. Roll each out to a saucer size. Place a good spoonful of the filling on one half. Fold over the dough to make a half-moon and pinch the edges together well.

7) Place all the turnovers in the heated roasting pans and cook in the oven for 10 minutes, turning once, until browned and crisp.

Sweet Potato Empanadas

Makes 12

U se leftover cold sweet potatoes for these delicious parcels. If you haven't any, use or-dinary cooked potatoes, carrots or even parsnips. To use raw sweet potatoes, peel, dice and cook quickly in a little boiling water until tender. They can cook while you are making the dough.

Filling
1 tablespoon oil
1 small onion, finely chopped
1 serrano chili, finely chopped
1 tablespoon ground almonds
1 tablespoon raisins
2 cups cooked sweet potatoes, diced
1 teaspoon ground cinnamon

salt and pepper

Dough
¾ cup boiling water
¼ cup soft butter or margarine
½ teaspoon salt
2½ cups flour

oil for deep-frying

1) In a large skillet sauté the onion and chili in the oil over moderate heat, stirring, for a couple of minutes. Add the almonds and raisins. Cook for 1 minute.
2) Add the sweet potatoes and cinnamon and season well with salt and pepper.
3) Put all the dough ingredients into a food processor with a dough attachment and process until a soft dough is formed.
4) Divide the dough into 12 balls and roll each out to about a 7¼-inch circle.
5) Place a spoonful of filling on each half and fold over, pinching the edges very well.

6) In a deep, heavy skillet or kettle, heat about 3 inches oil over moderately high heat to 375°F on a deep-fat thermometer. Gently drop the empanadas, in batches, into the oil and fry, turning, until crisp and golden.

Cook's Note

These empanadas can also be baked as in Chard and Spinach Empanadas, page 46.

Chili Non Carne

Serves 4–6

*T*his is a basic, very easy chili, otherwise known in TexMex parlance as a bowl of red. Serve it with tortillas, rice or bread. Canned hominy grits or instant polenta also make good substantial foils for it. Serve with sour cream or cheese if desired.

2 tablespoons vegetable oil
2 cups mushrooms
2 medium onions, peeled and quartered
2 cloves garlic, peeled
1 medium poblano chili, seeded

14 oz canned red kidney beans, rinsed and drained
14 oz canned chopped tomatoes
salt and pepper

1) Place the oil, mushrooms, onions, garlic and chili into a food processor. Using the pulse button, chop until finely minced.

2) Scrape into a heavy skillet. Cook over high heat, stirring, until browned.

3) Add the kidney beans. Cook for 2 minutes and then add the tomatoes. Simmer for 10 minutes. Season and serve.

Chimichangas

Makes 6

A tasty way of using up the Chili leftovers. If you haven't any, use a mixture of cooked vegetables. Broccoli and sweet corn with a dash of sour cream and a sprinkle of coarsely ground chili powder is good.

Serve with a good dollop of sour cream, some shredded lettuce and Guacamole III (see page 25).

2 cups of leftover chili or cooked vegetables	6 flour tortillas oil for frying

1) Place a good spoonful of the filling in the center of each tortilla. Fold the bottom of the tortilla over the filling. Fold in the sides. Fold down the top to form a parcel. Secure with a toothpick.

2) In a deep, large heavy skillet, heat about ½ inch oil over moderately high heat. Carefully fry the tortillas, turning, until crisp and golden on both sides.

Enchiladas Suizas

Makes 12

*U*nctuous, utterly delicious and . . . fattening. Go on, indulge yourself occasionally. Placate your conscience by filling up on lots of fresh salad vegetables.

1 small bunch spring onions (scallions), chopped
2 cloves garlic, chopped
3 cups mushrooms, preferably oyster and button, sliced
1 tablespoon butter or oil
1¼ cups crème fraîche (available at specialty food shops and some supermarkets)

2 cups crushed tomatoes
1 canned jalapeño, chopped
4 tomatillos, chopped (use gherkins, if unavailable)
salt and pepper
12 corn tortillas
oil
1 cup mozzarella, grated

1) In a skillet sauté the spring onions (scallions), garlic and mushrooms briefly in the butter over moderate heat.
2) Add ¼ cup of the crème fraîche and stir. Remove from heat.
3) In a bowl mix together the tomatoes, jalapeño, tomatillos and the remaining crème fraîche. Season.
4) In a skillet briefly fry the tortillas in a little oil over moderate heat so they become pliable. Dip a tortilla into the tomato sauce, spoon a dollop of the mushroom mixture in the center and roll up.

5) Lay in a large baking pan and repeat, filling all the tortillas. Pour over the rest of the sauce. Cover with the mozzarella and bake in a preheated 400°F oven for 12 minutes. Serve immediately.

Enchiladas

Makes 12

*L*ess rich than the Enchiladas Suiza (see page 52), this is a more run-of-the-mill dish, but good. I have used eggplant strips instead of chicken, but you can use zucchini, mushrooms or whatever you fancy.

1 large eggplant, cut into strips
2 cloves garlic, crushed
2 tablespoons oil
½ teaspoon ground cumin
⅓ cup plain yogurt or sour
  cream
salt and pepper
1 onion, chopped
1 clove garlic, chopped
2 serrano chilies, chopped

1 small green bell pepper,
  chopped
14 oz can chopped tomatoes
12 corn tortillas
oil
½ cup *chèvre sec* (aged goat
  cheese) or, if unavailable, feta
  cheese, crumbled
2 spring onions (scallions),
  chopped (optional)

1) In a skillet cook the eggplant and crushed garlic in 1 tablespoon of the oil over moderate heat, stirring, until browned and softened. Add the cumin and yogurt or sour cream. Season and remove from heat.

2) In a separate skillet sauté the onion, garlic, chilies and bell pepper in remaining 1 tablespoon of oil over moderate heat, stirring, until softened. Add the tomatoes. Cook over high heat, stirring, until slightly thickened. Remove from heat.

3) In another skillet, fry the tortillas very briefly in a little oil over moderate heat so they become pliable.

4) Fill the tortillas with the eggplant mixture, roll them up and place them in a baking dish.

5) Cover with the tomato sauce, sprinkle with the cheese and cover tightly with foil. Bake in a preheated 400°F oven for 10 minutes.

6) Scatter the spring onions (scallions) over the enchiladas and serve.

Enchiladas with Sweet Potato

Makes 12

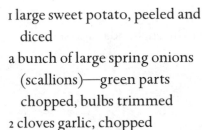

1 large sweet potato, peeled and
    diced
a bunch of large spring onions
    (scallions)—green parts
    chopped, bulbs trimmed
2 cloves garlic, chopped
2 tablespoons oil

juice from 1 lime
salt and pepper
1–2 jalapeños, finely chopped
2 cups crushed tomatoes
12 corn tortillas, steamed
½ cup dry ricotta or feta
    cheese, crumbled

1) In a skillet cook the sweet potato, spring onions (scallions) and garlic in the oil over moderate heat, stirring, until softened. Add the lime juice. Season. Remove from heat.

2) In a bowl mix together the jalapeño and tomatoes.

3) Dip the tortillas in the tomato mixture.

4) Fill each tortilla with some sweet potato mixture, roll up and lay in a baking dish. Pour over the remaining tomatoes. Top with the cheese and bake in a preheated 400°F oven for 10 minutes.

Fajitas

Makes 6

*F*ajitas actually means sashes. The term refers to the way the food (usually beef) is cut into strips. This recipe calls for eggplant, but large flat mushrooms or zucchini, even bell peppers, can be used.

juice from 1 lime

2 medium eggplants, halved
   and thinly sliced lengthways

1 tablespoon all-purpose flour
   mixed with 1 teaspoon
   coarsely ground dried chili

oil

6 large flour tortillas, warmed

½ a tray of Roasted Peppers (see
   page 97)

2 ripe avocados, peeled and
   sliced

1 serrano chili, finely chopped

coriander (cilantro)

1) In a bowl, pour the lime juice over the eggplant. Dust with the flour and chili.

2) In a skillet cook the eggplant in hot oil, in batches, over moderate heat until nicely browned.

3) Fill the tortillas with the eggplant and Roasted Peppers. Top with the avocado, sprinkled with the chopped chili and a sprig of coriander (cilantro). Serve.

Flautas con Calabacitas

Makes 12

Zucchini are cut into strips before being rolled inside corn tortillas.

oil
2 cloves garlic, chopped
1 canned jalapeño, sliced
4 cups zucchini, cut in julienne
   strips
a pinch of salt
a generous grinding of black
   pepper

juice of ½ a lime
12 corn tortillas
3 tablespoons grated parmesan
   or mahon cheese
chunky tomato salsa

1) In a skillet heat 2 tablespoons of oil over moderate heat. Add the garlic and chili and cook until the garlic colors. Add the zucchini and stir-fry until just tender—this does not take long.

2) Add salt and pepper and the lime juice.

3) Divide the mixture between the tortillas and roll up tightly.

4) In a large skillet cook the tortillas in hot oil over moderate heat until crisp and golden. Dust with the cheese and serve with a chunky salsa.

Gorditas

Makes 12

Their name means "little fatties" and they are a thicker tortilla. Almost like hoecakes, these cornmeal griddlecakes can be filled with most things from simple grated cheese to tomato sauces to leftover Chili (see page 50).

1 cup instant polenta (precooked cornmeal)	1 serrano chili, finely chopped
2 cups water	1 cup ricotta cheese
½ teaspoon salt	oil
1 teaspoon double-acting baking powder	½ head iceberg lettuce, shredded
1 teaspoon margarine	tomato salsa

1) In a nonstick pan cook the polenta, water, salt, baking powder and margarine over low heat, stirring, until the mixture leaves the pan's sides easily. This takes only a few minutes.
2) Divide into 12 balls. Flatten each in turn on a sheet of baking paper and turn onto heated griddle or dry skillet. Cook, turning until a crust develops on both sides.
3) In a small bowl mix the chili into the ricotta.
4) In a heavy frying pan or skillet heat the oil over moderate heat. Fry the cornmeal cakes until golden and slightly puffed.
5) Drain and slit open. Fill with ricotta and lettuce. Serve immediately with a tomato salsa.

Mexican Lasagne

Serves 4–6

Here's another recipe for a baked dish. Like the Black Beans in Beer (see page 42), the tomato sauce is layered with tortillas. In some places this is known as *Budin*.

3 tablespoons oil
8 corn tortillas
1 onion, roughly chopped
2 cloves garlic, chopped
a small can tomatillos, drained
   and chopped—use a few
   gherkins if unavailable
3 cups crushed tomatoes
2 tablespoons chopped

coriander (cilantro)
1 scant cup crème fraîche
   (available in specialty food
   shops and some supermarkets)
1 cup fresh mozzarella, torn
3 pasado chilies, sliced (or an-
   choes, roasted and sliced)

1) In a skillet cook the tortillas in the oil over moderate heat. Reserve. In the same skillet cook the onion, garlic and tomatillos. Add the tomatoes. Stir over a high heat for 2 minutes. Season and add the coriander (cilantro).

2) In a deep heatproof dish lay a couple of tortillas. Cover with some of the tomato sauce, then some of the crème fraîche, the mozzarella and then a sprinkle of chilies. Repeat the layers until all is used up. Bake in a preheated 400°F oven for 20 minutes and serve.

Papadzules

Makes 6

Enchiladas from the Yucatan: these tortillas are filled with eggs and pumpkin seed sauce and dressed with Chiltomate, a fiery tomato sauce. Those of feebler temperament are advised to swap the habanero chilies for something less hot.

6 corn tortillas, steamed to
warm

Mole Pepitas (see page 28)

6 hard-boiled eggs, peeled and
chopped

Chiltomate (see page 22)

1) Spread the tortillas with the Mole Pepitas, sprinkle with hard-boiled eggs and roll up. Spoon over the Chiltomate and warm in a preheated 400°F oven for 7–10 minutes.

Panuchos

Makes 6

This is another recipe from the Yucatan. The traditional method calls for a pocket to be made in the tortilla. Commercially available uncooked tortillas seem unwilling to open themselves up like this. Therefore, these quick panuchos are a sandwich of two tortillas. I am relieved to discover from the authoritative *Authentic Mexican Cooking* by Rick and Deann Bayless that this is accepted practice in some places.

oil
1 onion, chopped
1 serrano chili, chopped
14 oz can black beans, rinsed and drained
12 small thin corn tortillas
2 hard-boiled eggs, sliced
3 tomatoes, peeled and chopped

1 canned jalapeño, thinly sliced
1 head romaine lettuce, shredded
2 small jars Italian antipasti—cipolline in agrodolce and insalata di funghi (onions and mushrooms)

1) In a skillet cook the onion and serrano chili in 4 tablespoons of oil over moderate heat. Add the beans and crush with the back of the spoon while stirring.

2) Spread a good spoonful of bean mixture on 6 tortillas. Top with the egg slices and then press a second tortilla on top.

3) In another skillet cook the tortilla sandwiches in some oil over moderate heat, turning until golden on both sides.

4) In a small bowl mix together the tomatoes and the jalapeño.
5) Serve the tortillas garnished with a spoon of the tomato and chili mixture, lettuce and the Italian onions and mushrooms.

Pepián

Serves 4–6

This is a creamy corn-based stew. This version contains oyster mushrooms instead of the more usual pork. Serve with rice.

4 tablespoons oil

4 cups oyster mushrooms, cut in strips

2 onions, chopped

2 pasado chilies, chopped

2 cloves garlic, chopped

14 oz creamed sweet corn

⅓ cup evaporated milk plus extra if required

salt and pepper

a bunch of fresh coriander (cilantro), chopped

1) In a skillet sauté the mushrooms quickly in 2 tablespoons of the oil over moderate heat until browned. Set aside.

2) Cook the onions and chilies in the remaining 2 tablespoons of oil until browned. Add the garlic. Cook for 1 minute. Add the sweet corn and evaporated milk.

3) Lower heat and season well with salt and pepper.

4) Simmer for 5 minutes, adding a little more evaporated milk if too thick. Add the mushrooms and coriander (cilantro). Simmer a couple of minutes longer and serve.

Tortilla Flats

Makes 6

See the recipe for Refried Beans (see page 7) or use canned variety.

4 tablespoons vegetable oil
3 cups refried beans
six 7-inch flour tortillas
2 cups double Gloucester or
   Monterey Jack cheese, grated
½ head iceberg lettuce,
   shredded
2 ripe avocados, sliced

Pepper Salsa or Salsa Cruda—
   homemade (see pages 32 and
   35) or store-bought

1) In a heavy skillet fry the beans in the oil over moderate heat, making 6 "cakes."
2) Warm the tortillas in the oven.
3) Slide each bean "cake" onto a tortilla. Sprinkle with cheese. Top with the lettuce, avocado slices and a spoonful of salsa. Serve immediately.

Red Beans and Pepitas

Serves 4–6

Pepitas are, in this instance, pumpkin seeds. Find the smooth pale green ovals of shelled seeds in natural food stores and by mail order from Sultan's Delight, tel. 800-852-5046.

1 cup pumpkin seeds, toasted
1 teaspoon ancho powder
1 teaspoon pasilla powder
1 tablespoon ground cumin
1 tablespoon brown sugar
2 onions, chopped
4 cloves garlic, crushed
8 large flat mushrooms
2 tablespoons oil

14 oz. can chopped tomatoes
7 oz. sweet corn kernels
bunch of spring onions
  (scallions), chopped
14 oz. can red kidney beans,
  rinsed and drained
2 tablespoons tomato purée
  mixed with 1 cup hot water
salt and pepper

1) In a food processor process the pumpkin seeds, reserving a handful for topping. When coarsely ground, mix together with the chili powders, cumin and sugar.
2) In a skillet cook the onions, garlic and mushrooms in the oil over moderate heat until browned. Add the pumpkin seed mix. Stir and add the tomatoes, sweet corn, most of the spring onions (scallions), leaving a handful for the top, the beans and the tomato purée mixture.
3) Simmer for 10 minutes, adding more water if necessary.
4) Season to taste and top with the reserved seeds and spring onions (scallions).
5) Serve with flour tortillas or rice and a bowl of sour cream.

Tostadas

Makes 12

The toppings can be altered to accommodate what you have available. In this recipe, use canned Frijoles Refritos or your own leftovers (see page 7). As Tostadas are so simple and so good, there are three variations on this theme. Try them all, then make up your own.

1 tablespoon oil
a good pinch of cumin seeds
4 black peppercorns, crushed
1 bay leaf
oregano
a small piece of lime zest
salt
1 red onion, sliced
2 cloves garlic, sliced
1 canned jalapeño chili,
   chopped

2 cups sliced oyster mushrooms
2 tablespoons water
twelve 4-inch corn tortillas,
   fried crisp
2 cups Frijoles Refritos,
   reheated (see page 7)
¾ cup crème fraîche
coriander (cilantro)

1) In a skillet heat the oil and in it sauté the cumin and peppercorns over moderate heat. Add the bay leaf, oregano, the lime zest, a good pinch of salt, onion, garlic, chili and mushrooms. Cook quickly for 1 minute, then add the water and cook 5 minutes, until just tender.

2) Spread each tortilla with Frijoles Refritos, top with the mushroom mixture and finish with a good spoonful of crème fraîche and a sprig of coriander (cilantro).

Broccoli and Black Bean Tostadas

Makes 12

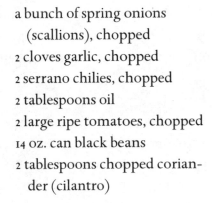

a bunch of spring onions
(scallions), chopped
2 cloves garlic, chopped
2 serrano chilies, chopped
2 tablespoons oil
2 large ripe tomatoes, chopped
14 oz. can black beans
2 tablespoons chopped coriander (cilantro)

salt and pepper
twelve 4-inch corn tortillas,
fried crisp
3 cups barely cooked broccoli
florets
Guacamole II (see page 24) or ½
cup sour cream and 1 large
avocado, sliced
dried chili flakes (optional)

1) In a skillet cook the spring onions (scallions), garlic and chilies in the oil over moderate heat.

2) Add the tomatoes and black beans and cook until thick. Stir in the coriander (cilantro). Season.

3) Spoon the black bean mixture onto the tortillas. Top with the broccoli and Guacamole or sour cream and avocado. Sprinkle with chili flakes if desired. Serve.

Potato Tostadas

Makes 12

*U*nlike the two previous recipes there are no beans on these tostadas—their place is taken by a fragrant potato mixture similar to a curry.

2 tablespoons oil	2 tomatoes, diced
2 guajillo chilies, soaked	1 cup fresh or frozen peas
1 New Mexico red chili, soaked	½ cup sweet corn kernels
1 onion, peeled and quartered	twelve 4-inch corn tortillas,
4 cloves garlic, peeled	fried crisp
1 lime	1 cup crumbled dry goat or
a good pinch of brown sugar	feta cheese
¼ teaspoon salt	1 serrano chili, finely shredded
2½ cups potatoes, diced	for garnish (optional)

1) In a food processor, mix the oil, guajillo and New Mexico red chilies, onion and garlic to make a paste.

2) In a skillet cook the paste for 1 minute over moderate heat. Add the juice and a little grated zest of the lime. Stir in the sugar, salt, and potatoes. Stir for about 1 minute. Add the tomatoes.

3) Cook covered until the potatoes are tender, adding a little water if necessary to prevent sticking.

4) Add the peas and sweet corn and cook for another 3 minutes.

5) Spoon onto the corn tortillas. Top with the cheese and serrano if using.

Blue Corn Eggplant
à la Veracruzana

Serves 4–6

This is a contrived dish in that Veracruzan sauce is more properly served with fish. There is an almost Mediterranean flavor to this dish. Blue corn is just another variety of ground maize; you can use ordinary golden cornmeal instead—the flavor will not suffer.

1 very large or 2 medium egg-plants—cut into 8 long slices	1 jalapeño, sliced
salt	1 tablespoon coriander (cilantro), chopped
2 medium onions, chopped	1 bay leaf
2 cloves garlic, crushed	a good pinch ground cloves
2 tablespoons olive oil	½ teaspoon ground cinnamon
2 small green bell peppers, sliced	black pepper
28 oz can chopped tomatoes	1 cup blue cornmeal
½ cup green olives, chopped	oil or butter to fry
½ cup capers	1 lime

1) Sprinkle the eggplant slices with salt.
2) In a skillet cook the onion, garlic and green bell peppers in the oil over moderate heat for 5 minutes.

3) Add the tomatoes, olives, capers, jalapeño, coriander (cilantro), bay leaf and spices. Season well with black pepper and salt.

4) Simmer for 15 minutes, stirring occasionally and adding a little water if the sauce becomes too thick and begins to stick.

5) Scrape the salt off the eggplants.

6) Coat the slices on both sides with cornmeal and shallow-fry in hot oil over moderately high heat until crisp and deep purple (nicely browned if using ordinary cornmeal).

7) Serve with the sauce and wedges of lime.

Eggs and Cheese

Chile Queso

Serves 4–6

Cheese-stuffed chilies. The best chilies to use for this are poblano but, as with the Chiles Rellenos (see page 43), if you can't bear things too hot, stuff a green bell pepper instead.

6 poblano chilies (see above)
2 cups mild feta cheese, crumbled
a little oil

3 tomatoes, skinned and chopped
4 tablespoons tortilla chips, crushed

1) Cut the chilies in half lengthways and remove the seeds. Fill with the cheese.
2) Pour a little oil into a shallow baking dish. Add the tomatoes and arrange the chilies on top, cut side up.
3) Sprinkle each with the tortilla crumbs and bake in a preheated 400°F oven for 20 minutes. Serve with tortillas or rice and an avocado salad.

Crepas con Elote

Serves 4–6

*T*his is really a TexMex variant. Serve for breakfast, lunch or supper. Top with fillings if desired.

4 eggs, separated	2 teaspoons baking soda
4 tablespoons melted butter or margarine	1 teaspoon salt
10 oz. can creamed corn	1 tablespoon brown sugar
1 cup buttermilk or ½ cup milk and ½ cup sour cream	3 canned jalapeño chilies, sliced
2 cups cornmeal	2 tomatoes, chopped
	1 onion, finely chopped
	oil or butter for cooking

1) In a bowl beat the egg yolks with the butter, creamed corn and buttermilk.
2) In another bowl, whisk the egg whites until stiff.
3) Sift together the baking soda and salt.
4) In a large bowl combine all the ingredients gently.
5) Heat a little oil or butter on a seasoned griddle or heavy skillet. Cook 3-inch pancakes, turning carefully to lightly brown both sides.

Chiles en Nogado

Serves 4–6

This dish of stuffed chilies is especially served on Mexico's Independence Day. It has the colors of the Mexican flag: green, white and red. If you don't like things *muy piccante*, use sweet green bell peppers instead.

2 large onions, finely chopped
2 cloves garlic, crushed
2 tablespoons vegetable oil
2 tablespoons raisins
½ teaspoon ground cumin
2 cups bread crumbs
1 egg, beaten
salt and pepper
4 large green chilies, halved
   lengthways and seeded

Either
¼ cup sour cream

or
1¼ cups milk
2 teaspoons flour
2 teaspoons butter or
   margarine

1 cup walnuts, chopped
1 pomegranate

1) In a skillet cook the onion and garlic in the oil over moderate heat. When golden, add the raisins, cumin and bread crumbs.
2) Remove from the heat; bind with the egg. Season with salt and pepper.
3) Press into the chili halves and invert in a baking dish.
4) If using sour cream, simply mix in the walnuts and spoon over. Otherwise in a saucepan whisk together the milk, flour and butter over low heat until thickened.

5) Add the walnuts and pour over the chilies.

6) Bake in a preheated 400°F oven for 20 minutes. Top with the pomegranate seeds. Serve.

Entomatadas

Makes 12

*F*aster than the other two Enchilada recipes, this is much more of a TexMex variant, though it is found in the north of Mexico.

14 oz can chopped tomatoes	12 corn tortillas
1 onion, quartered	oil
2 cloves garlic, crushed	4 cups grated cheddar or
3 serrano chilies	münster cheese
2 tablespoons oil	

1) In a food processor or blender process the tomatoes, onion, garlic and chilies until puréed.

2) In a skillet cook the purée in the oil over moderate heat, stirring for 3 minutes. (Watch out for spattering.)

3) In another skillet cook the tortillas briefly to make them pliable.

4) Roll up the tortillas with grated cheese inside—reserving some cheese to sprinkle on the top.

5) Place tortillas in a shallow baking dish. Cover with the sauce. Add the cheese topping.

6) Cover with foil and bake in a preheated 400°F oven for 10 minutes. Serve.

Flautas con Queso Fresco

Makes 12

*T*hese crisp, delicious tortillas tightly rolled with fresh cheese remind me of the Turk-ish Sigara Börek—often weirdly translated as cigarette pie! Eat the flautas (flutes) as snacks or make a Chiltomate sauce (see page 22) and pour it over the hot flautas and serve with a salad and/or Guacamole (see pages 23–25).

12 corn tortillas

oil

1¼ cups soft goat cheese or
   ricotta

1) Lay out the tortillas. Place a line of cheese on each one. Roll up.
2) In a heavy skillet heat ⅓ inch oil over moderate heat until hot but not smoking. Cook the rolled tortillas, a few at a time, until crisp and golden. Serve.

Cook's Note

Chopped canned chilies, spring onions (scallions) or coriander (cilantro) can be added to the cheese before filling the tortillas.

Huevos Motuleños

Serves 4–6

In the original Mexican dish, ham is used. Here, sun-dried tomato strips give that salty tang.

14 oz canned chopped tomatoes	sugar
2–4 serrano chilies, finely sliced	6 flour or corn tortillas
2 cloves garlic, crushed	6 eggs
1 small onion, chopped	4 sun-dried tomatoes, cut into slivers
vegetable oil	6 tablespoons grated cheddar
a pinch of cumin	or Monterey Jack cheese or
salt	cottage cheese

1) In a food processor or blender process the tomatoes, chilies, and garlic briefly.
2) In a skillet cook the onion in 2 tablespoons of oil. When lightly browned, stir in the tomato mixture. Season to taste with the cumin, salt and sugar. Simmer until thickened.
3) In another skillet cook the tortillas in a little oil over moderate heat so they become pliable and keep warm in the oven.
4) In the same skillet fry the eggs, adding the sun-dried tomatoes at the last moment.
5) Place the eggs on the tortillas. Cover with the tomato sauce and top with the cheese. Serve.

Huevos Rancheros

Serves 1

*F*ried eggs Mexican style. Use either your own pepper salsa or a good commercially prepared one.

1 small flour or corn tortilla per person	1 egg per person
vegetable oil	1–2 tablespoons Pepper Salsa (see page 32) per person

1) In a skillet cook the tortillas in some oil and keep warm in the oven.
2) In the skillet fry the eggs. Place an egg on each tortilla and serve topped with the Hot Pepper Salsa.
3) Decorate if desired with fresh coriander (cilantro) and/or avocado.

Huevos Revueltos

Serves 4–6

Scrambled eggs, but *"estilo mexicano"* (Mexican-fashion). Eat these tasty eggs for breakfast, lunch or supper. Roll them up in soft tortillas or serve with crusty rolls.

⅓ cup butter or shortening
1 onion, chopped
2 cloves garlic, chopped
1 jalapeño chili, chopped
1 large tomato, seeded and
   chopped

8 eggs, lightly beaten
salt and pepper

1) In a large skillet melt the butter over moderate heat. Add the onion, garlic, chili and tomato and cook for a few minutes. Stir in the eggs and season. Keep stirring until the eggs are just set and serve immediately.

Mexican Cheese on Tortilla

Serves 4–6

Almost as quick as cheese on toast, this recipe uses flour tortillas and ready-made sauces. You can of course use your own salsa (see pages 31–35), but this will increase the preparation time.

1 serrano chili, chopped	2 cups Monterey Jack or mild
2½ cups mushrooms, chopped	cheddar cheese, grated
1 tablespoon oil	1 jar pepper salsa
3 large flour tortillas	

1) In a skillet cook the chili and mushrooms in the oil over moderate heat until browned.
2) Scatter the mixture over the tortillas and sprinkle with the cheese.
3) Bake in a preheated 450°F oven for 8 minutes or until the edges are crisp. Serve, cut into wedges, with a spoonful of salsa.

Mexican Corn Pudding

Serves 4—6

a small, stale loaf of bread, cubed

14 oz can sweet corn

2 large eggs, beaten

½ cup milk

salt and pepper

2 canned jalapeño chilies, finely chopped

2 spring onions (scallions), sliced

¼ cup finely grated cheddar or Monterey Jack cheese

Pepper Salsa (see page 32)

1) In a bowl mix together the bread, sweet corn, eggs and milk. Season with salt and pepper. Add the chilies and spring onions (scallions).

2) Pour mixture into a greased 9-inch square baking dish.

3) Sprinkle with the cheese and bake in a preheated 375°F oven for 20 minutes. Serve cut into squares with a Pepper Salsa.

Nopales and Egg

Serves 4–6

*T*his is another version of Huevos Revueltos (see page 82). If you cannot get nopales—cactus stems—use steamed broccoli stems with a squeeze of lime juice. Not the same, but still tasty.

1 onion, chopped
1 canned jalapeño chili, cut
   into thin strips
2 tablespoons oil or butter
1 tomato, roughly chopped

12 oz. jar or can cactus pieces
   empty into a sieve and run
   under the tap for a minute,
   then slice
8 eggs, lightly beaten with a
   little salt

1) In a skillet cook the onion and chili in the oil over moderate heat until softened. Add the tomato and cactus pieces. Cook until softened. Add the eggs and stir until the eggs are just set. Serve immediately with warm tortillas.

Quesadillas

Serves 4–6

Sauce
2 teaspoons ancho powder
7 oz can chopped tomatoes
1 small onion, roughly
   chopped
2 cloves garlic, crushed
1 tablespoon oil
a good pinch brown sugar
salt and pepper

1 tablespoon chopped parsley
a squeeze of lime

4 flour tortillas
1¼ cups crumbled feta cheese
4 spring onions (scallions),
   chopped
a little oil

1) Place the ancho powder, tomatoes, onion and garlic in a blender or food processor and process briefly.

2) In a skillet cook the paste in the oil over moderate heat for 5 minutes, stirring. Add the sugar, and season with salt and pepper. Add the parsley and lime.

3) Spread a spoon of the tomato sauce over half a tortilla. Cover with cheese and spring onion (scallion). Fold over to make a half moon shape. In another skillet cook the tortillas in a very little oil over moderate heat until cooked on both sides.

4) Cut into triangles to serve.

Cook's Note

Bottled sauces can be used for speed. If desired try with münster or mozzarella cheese (diced finely).

Queso Fundido

Serves 4–6

Queso fundido is essentially melted cheese as in a Swiss or French fondue—indeed, if you have a fondue set, you can melt the cheese carefully over the burner at the table. Widely available cheeses have been substituted for the authentic Mexican ones, but if you live near an esoteric deli, try asking for *Queso de Oaxaca* or *Queso de Chihuahua*.

2 ancho (dried poblano) chilies, dry roasted and crumbled

3 spring onions (scallions), chopped

1 tablespoon coriander (cilantro), chopped

2 cups cubed cheese—a mixture of two or more of the following: mozzarella, münster, greve, Monterey Jack, Cheshire

8 corn or flour tortillas

1) In a bowl mix together the anchos, spring onions (scallions) and coriander (cilantro).
2) In a heatproof dish melt the cheese in a preheated 350°F oven until bubbling.
3) Sprinkle the chili mixture over the cheese and serve.
4) Diners scoop out cheese and roll it up in tortillas to eat—messy but delicious. Serve with a fresh salsa and some oven-roasted peppers, tomatoes and zucchini.

Vegetables and salads

Ejote con Tortilla

Serves 4–6

Beans aren't the only vegetables you could use for this very simple dish: cauliflower, broccoli, zucchini and snow peas all work well.

2 cloves garlic, crushed
1 small onion, chopped
2 tablespoons oil
1 serrano chili, seeded and
  finely chopped
6 cups green beans, cut into
  1-inch lengths

½ cup water or tomato juice
salt and pepper
a pinch of sugar
2 tablespoons chopped
  coriander (cilantro)
2 tablespoons broken tortilla
  chips

1) In a skillet cook the garlic and onion in the oil over moderate heat. Add chili and beans. Cook, covered, for a couple of minutes over moderate heat, shaking the pan occasionally.

2) Pour in the water or tomato juice. Season with salt, pepper and a pinch of sugar.

3) Cover and simmer until the beans are tender—about 10 minutes.

4) Stir through the coriander (cilantro) and sprinkle over the crushed tortilla chips. Serve immediately.

Elote

Serves 4–6

This is simply corn on the cob. When next barbecuing, throw some sweet corn on the grill rack and serve it this way.

6 sweet corn on the cob	½ teaspoon dried crushed red
1 lime, cut into wedges	chilies
2 tablespoons butter	a good pinch of salt

1) In a large kettle boil the corn in plenty of *unsalted* water for 7 minutes. Drain.
2) Rub each corn with a wedge of lime. Serve with the butter and sprinkle with the chili and salt.

Cook's Note

If you have time, work the chili and salt into the butter. Chill well, then serve cut into pats with the corn.

Ensalada à la Mexicana

Serves 4–6

*T*his is really Mexico through U.S. eyes as salad south of the border is more like a chutney or relish. However questionable its antecedents, this is a great salad. The vinaigrette is fiery. If you want to temper its heat, choose a milder chili.

1 large head romaine lettuce, shredded

a small bunch of arugula

1½ cups coriander (cilantro)

1 cup radishes, sliced

2 habanero chilies, quartered and seeded

a small bunch of spring onions (scallions), roughly chopped

12 oz. can tomatillos, rinsed and drained

¾ cup good corn or olive oil

juice of 1 lime

2 tablespoons light brown sugar

⅓ cup of boiling water

1 small red onion, finely chopped

2 corn tortillas, fried crisp and crumbled

½ cup feta cheese, crumbled

1) In a large salad bowl mix together the romaine, arugula, coriander (cilantro) and radishes.

2) In a food processor put the chilies, spring onions (scallions) and tomatillos and chop to a very rough purée with the pulse button. Add the oil, lime juice, sugar and boiling water and process at a high speed for a few seconds.

3) Pour over the salad. Sprinkle with the red onion, tortilla crumbs and the feta. Serve immediately.

Ensalada de Aguacate

Serves 4–6

A vocado salad with a kick. Use this salad as a side dish or use it to stuff flour tortillas with a handful of crumbled feta cheese.

½ head iceberg lettuce, shredded

3 ripe avocados, peeled and sliced

2 tablespoons chopped coriander (cilantro)

1–2 guajillo chilies, dry roasted and crumbled

1 clove garlic, crushed

1 small onion, chopped

salt and pepper

oil

1) Line a salad dish or plate with the lettuce. Cover with the avocado slices.
2) In a small bowl mix together the coriander (cilantro), chilies, garlic and onion. Sprinkle over the salad. Season then drizzle with oil to taste.

Hongos à la Mexicana

Serves 4–6

Mexican mushrooms, well . . . mushrooms in a Mexican style. This is good with soft corn or wheat flour tortillas to mop up those gorgeous juices.

2 fresh poblano chilies, halved
 and seeded
2 onions, chopped
2 cloves garlic, chopped
2 tablespoons oil
6 cups large open flat field
 mushrooms, cut into chunks
1 tablespoon chopped celery
 leaves or use celery salt to
 season

2 cups crushed tomatoes
a sprig of thyme
½ teaspoon dried oregano
a sprig of rosemary
1 bay leaf
salt and pepper
1 cup water or vegetable stock

1) Roast the poblanos as indicated on page 97 until the skins blacken. When the peppers are cool enough to handle, peel and chop roughly.
2) In a skillet cook the onion and garlic in the oil over moderate heat until browned. Add the mushrooms. Cook, stirring, over moderately high heat for 5 minutes. Add the celery leaves and tomatoes. Cook for 4 minutes, stirring.
3) Add the remaining ingredients, seasoning well. Simmer until thick. Serve.

Jícama Salad

Serves 4–6

Jícama looks like a pale brown beetroot and has a crisp flesh. It makes a lovely, juicy and refreshing salad—celeriac can be substituted if required.

1 head romaine lettuce
1 lb jícama, peeled and sliced
  into half-moons
1 medium papaya, peeled,
  halved, seeded and sliced
1 cucumber, halved lengthways, seeded and sliced
2 spring onions (scallions),
  chopped

Dressing
the rind and juice of 1 lime
4 tablespoons oil
1 crushed clove garlic
a good pinch of salt
a pinch of sugar
1 dried pequín chili, crumbled
  or chopped

1) Line a bowl or salad plate with the lettuce leaves. Arrange the jícama, papaya and cucumber slices over the lettuce. Scatter over the spring onions (scallions). Shake the dressing ingredients together in a screw-topped jar and pour over the salad. Serve.

Pattypan Squash

Serves 4–6

*I*f you can get the baby squashes, use them whole. If no pattypan (summer squash) are available, use other types of squash including marrow, zucchini, butternut and pumpkin. Serve with rice and grated cheese as a full meal or use as a side dish or tortilla filling.

1 large onion, chopped

3 cloves garlic, crushed

2 tablespoons vegetable oil

2 serrano chilies, seeded and finely shredded

4 cups pattypan squash, cut into 1-inch chunks

3 large tomatoes, chopped or 7 oz canned chopped tomatoes

1 green bell pepper, seeded and chopped

salt and pepper

1) In a skillet cook the onion and garlic in the oil over moderately high heat until softened. Add the rest of the ingredients. Cook, stirring, over moderate heat for 5 minutes and then cover tightly.

2) Turn heat to low and cook a further 15 minutes.

3) Season with salt and pepper. If desired, add a handful of chopped coriander (cilantro) or parsley just before serving.

Cook's Note

This dish is equally good hot, tepid or well chilled.

Roasted Peppers

Serves 4–6

*T*his dish is very similar to the Spanish *Esclavida*. If you happen to be barbecuing, roast the peppers over the coals or crank the oven temperature up as high as it will go.

3 poblano chilies, seeded
3 serrano chilies, seeded
2 red bell peppers, quartered
   and seeded
1 yellow bell pepper, quartered
   and seeded
1 green bell pepper, quartered
   and seeded
4 small onions, peeled and
   trimmed

4 cloves garlic
oil
coarsely ground salt
freshly ground black pepper
a sprig of thyme
1 teaspoon dried oregano
a heaped cup crème fraîche

1) Place all the chilies and peppers in a heavy-duty baking tray with the onions and garlic. Drizzle over the oil. Sprinkle liberally with salt and pepper.
2) Broil until blackened and soft—about 15 minutes.
3) When the pepper are cool enough to handle, peel off the skins and roughly cut into chunks. Add the herbs and crème fraîche. Reheat and season if necessary.
4) Eat with soft tortillas or crusty rolls.

Snacks

Devilled Nuts

Serves 4–6

Much nicer than commercially available dry-roasted peanuts, these nuts are sold on the street in many Mexican cities. Use whichever nuts you like or have on hand. Pecans—native to Mexico—and almonds are especially good. Seeds, such as pumpkin or sunflower, can also be used as soy bean "splits" (toasted soy beans sold as snack food).

> 1 cup shelled peanuts   a good pinch of salt
> 1 teaspoon ground chili

1) In a skillet dry roast the peanuts over moderate heat, shaking the pan to toast them evenly. Sprinkle with the chili and salt. Shake for a few more seconds to evenly coat the nuts and serve when cooled.

Cook's Note

If desired, a few drops of lime juice can be squeezed over the nuts.

Jícama

Serves 4–6

Jícama is a root vegetable with the shape of a large Christmas bauble. It looks like a pale brown-skinned beet. The flavor is slightly sweetish, slightly fruity. If you are unable to find it, a good substitute for these crudités is celeriac—the turnip-rooted celery

2 teaspoons coarse sea salt
½ teaspoon coarsely ground
  cayenne pepper

2 cups jícama, peeled and cut
  into thin batons
juice of a lime

1) Mix together the sea salt and the cayenne.
2) Arrange the jícama on a plate. In the middle, place a deep saucer. Put the lime juice in the middle of the saucer and sprinkle the salt and cayenne around the edge of the plate. Diners dip the batons first in the lime juice and then in the salt and cayenne.

Nachos

Serves 4–6

14 oz. can refried beans or see page 7

1 large packet tortilla corn chips

2 medium tomatoes, peeled, seeded and diced

2 cups Monterey Jack or cheddar cheese, grated

2–3 canned jalapeños, thinly sliced

1) In a saucepan heat the beans over moderate heat. Spread some beans on each tortilla chip.

2) Lay out chips on a baking sheet.

3) Scatter over the tomato and cheese and top with a few slices of jalapeño. Heat for a few minutes in a preheated 400°F oven, until the cheese is bubbling and serve immediately.

Nopales Nibbles

Serves 4–6

A friend reports munching on nopales in a Mexican equivalent to a Spanish tapas bar. Serve this snack also as a side dish or salad.

1 onion, finely chopped	12 oz can or jar cactus pieces,
1 jalapeño, chopped	drained, rinsed and cubed
2 cloves garlic, crushed	salt and pepper
2 tablespoons oil	1 lime (optional)

1) In a skillet cook the onion, chili and garlic in the oil over moderate heat until softened but not colored.
2) Add the cactus pieces, tossing like a salad to coat in the fragrant oil. Season with salt (go easy), pepper and a squeeze of lime, if desired. Serve warm or cold.

Quick Sopes

Makes 18

This is a cheat's version of a favorite Mexican snack. It preserves the idea of the dish, but not its rather involved, labor-intensive production. The secret is to use cast iron muffin or popover pans, and to preheat them and the oven.

Don't be put off by the length of the list of ingredients—just choose one from the filling list and a couple from the toppings. It is a great way of using up leftovers and the scooped-out middles of the sopes can be used as dumplings in a soup or stew. Simply cool, pop into a bag and store in the freezer until required.

¾ cup cornmeal
¾ cup all-purpose flour
1 teaspoon baking powder
½ teaspoon salt
oil
2 eggs
1⅓ cups milk

chopped avocado and fresh
   chilies
ricotta cheese

(You'll need enough to fill 18
sopes—about 1 tablespoon
each.)

Fillings
Refried Beans, reheated (see
   page 7)
Huevos Revueltos, reheated
   (see page 82)
leftover chili, reheated

Toppings
1 jar cactus or tomato salsa
shredded lettuce
radish slices
coriander (cilantro)

1) Sift together the cornmeal, flour, baking powder and salt.

2) Pour a little oil into the bases of 18 muffin tins. Put in a preheated 450°F oven to heat.

3) Using a large whisk, in a bowl beat the eggs and milk into the cornmeal and flour mixture. Fill the muffin tins two-thirds full.

4) Bake 15 minutes until well risen and golden.

5) Turn out and scoop out the centers of the sopes with a melon baller. Do not scoop through the base. Reserve the middles for later use.

6) Fill the resulting cases with one of the fillings and add your chosen toppings. Serve immediately.

Tostaditas con Elote

Serves 4–6

This is such an easy dish to throw together. You can alter it by using Guacamole III (see page 25) instead of the tomato mixture. If you are in a hurry, choose a good quality ready-made tomato salsa. The colors are part of its charm—if you can find the rare blue corn tortillas, so much the better.

4 large tomatoes

2 spring onions (scallions), chopped

4 tomatillos, fresh or canned, chopped

2 tablespoons chopped coriander (cilantro)

salt and pepper

1 canned jalapeño, thinly sliced

2 cups sweet corn, canned or frozen

1 tablespoon melted butter

12 small corn tortillas, fried crisp

⅔ cup crème fraîche

1 serrano chili, finely sliced (optional)

1) Blacken the tomato skins—either in a gas flame or under a hot grill or broiler— and remove. Chop. Mix in the spring onions (scallions), tomatillos and coriander (cilantro). Season with salt and pepper.

2) In a skillet cook the jalapeño and sweet corn in the butter over moderate heat for 3 minutes.

3) On each tortilla place a layer of sweet corn, a spoonful of the tomato mixture, a teaspoon of crème fraîche and a slice of serrano. Reheat very briefly in a preheated 350°F oven on a baking sheet. Serve.

Pico de Gallo

Serves 4—6

Pico de gallo is found at roadside stalls and snack bars, but it makes a delicious appetizer or starter. It's perfect at a barbecue or an *alfresco* meal.

¼ of a watermelon, cubed

2 jícama, peeled and cubed

1 cucumber, cubed

4 small oranges, peeled and cut into eighths

4 apples, cored and cut into chunks

1 small pineapple, peeled and cubed

juice of 1 lime

a few mint leaves

1) In a large bowl mix everything together and serve with a jar of toothpicks, for diners to spear their chosen chunks.

Cook's Note

Avocado can also be added.

Desserts and Sweets

Atole de Almendrada

Serves 4–6

*E*at this cornmeal porridge for breakfast or as a comforting pudding.

Authentically, it is made with more water and used as a thick drink. My husband likened it to drinking knitting!

a scant ¼ cup instant polenta	1 cup milk
1 tablespoon ground almonds	1 teaspoon ground cinnamon
1 cup water	2–4 tablespoons brown sugar

1) In a saucepan mix everything together well and stir over moderate heat until the mixture thickens. Cook for 3 minutes. Serve.

Baked Tree Tomatoes

Serves 4–6

*T*ree Tomatoes, or *Tomate de arbol,* are more commonly found commercially labeled as tamarillos. This is the name ascribed to them by the New Zealand growers; they are, however, native to Central and South America. They can be eaten raw, but the fruit is sharply acidic. Baked, the flavor mellows and the color deepens.

4 tablespoons brown sugar	6 tamarillos, peeled and halved
2 teaspoons ground cinnamon	¼ cup butter

1) In a small bowl mix together the brown sugar and cinnamon.
2) Place the tamarillos in a baking dish, cut side up.
3) Sprinkle thickly with the sugar and cinnamon.
4) Dot with butter and bake in a preheated 350°F oven for 20 minutes.

Cabellero Pobre

Serves 4–6

*M*exican bread-and-butter pudding is usually flavored with cinnamon and raisins. To cut down on preparation time, this recipe uses the commercially available cinnamon raisin breads.

1 cup whole milk, warmed to just below a simmer	a small cinnamon and raisin loaf, cut into cubes
4 tablespoons sugar	zest of an orange
a few drops vanilla extract	3 eggs, beaten

1) In a bowl mix everything together very well.
2) Pour into a well-greased 9-inch square baking dish and bake in a preheated 350°F oven for 25 minutes.

Calabaza en Tacha

Serves 4–6

*P*umpkin in syrup! This is a Christmassy dish that can be eaten warm or chilled. You can bake or boil this simple but intriguing mixture. Serve with Flan (see page 118), cream or custard. If you can't get dried blueberries, simply omit this ingredient.

1 cup light brown sugar	a long strip of orange zest
1 cup water	4 cups pumpkin, cubed
2 tablespoons cider vinegar or	2 guavas, peeled and cubed
lime juice	1 orange, peeled and
2 sticks of cinnamon	segmented
2 cloves	1 tablespoon dried blueberries

1) In a saucepan melt the sugar in the water and vinegar or lime juice over low heat, stirring occasionally.
2) Add the spices and orange zest and bring to a boil. Cook for 3 minutes and then add the remaining ingredients.
3) Simmer gently or bake until the pumpkin and guava is tender—about 20 minutes.

Chocolate Cream

Serves 4–6

You can eat this grainy pudding warm or well chilled with a swirl of cream and a sprinkle of ground cinnamon.

1 cup dark chocolate, grated or in chips	1 teaspoon ground cinnamon
4⅓ cups whole milk	1 tablespoon dark rum
1 teaspoon finely grated orange rind	⅓ cup light brown sugar
	2 egg yolks
	2 tablespoons cornmeal

1) In a heavy-bottomed saucepan or a double boiler, melt the chocolate in half the milk, the orange rind and the cinnamon over low heat.

2) Stir in the rum. Add the sugar and stir well.

3) In a bowl beat the egg yolks with the cornmeal. Pour the egg mixture on the chocolate mixture. Beat in the remaining milk. Cook, stirring, until well thickened.

4) Serve immediately or set in small bowls in a cool place until well chilled.

Chongos

Serves 4–6

This is what Señorita Muffita would eat in Mexico before the tarantula comes down and really frightens her away—Chongos are curds and whey, and instead of rennet, lime juice is used to form the curds. This pudding takes no time to make, but improves with standing in a cool place before serving.

> 3 cups whole milk, warmed to 98°F
> 4 tablespoons superfine sugar
>
> 2 teaspoons ground cinnamon
> the juice of 1 lime

1) In the saucepan used to heat the milk, combine the milk with 3 tablespoons of the sugar and 1 teaspoon of cinnamon.
2) Slowly stir the lime juice into the milk, but don't whisk it or the curd will be all broken up. Pour into a chilled dish and put in the refrigerator before serving. Sprinkle with the remaining sugar and cinnamon mixed, together, before sending to the table.

Cook's Note

Rosewater is sometimes added to the milk for flavor. If you do this, send the dish to the table with a sprinkle of unsprayed rose petals.

Churros

Serves 4–6

Churros are a popular street food in Mexico as they are in Spain. Basically a choux paste that is deep-fried, they can be sweet or savory. If you want to try the latter, omit the sugar, add some hard cheese, such as mahon or parmesan, and dust with cayenne.

4 tablespoons confectioners' sugar	2¾ cups all-purpose flour
4 teaspoons ground cinnamon	4 tablespoons superfine sugar
2½ cups milk	2 eggs, well beaten
	oil for deep-frying

1) Sift the confectioners' sugar with the cinnamon into a bowl.
2) In a saucepan heat the milk over moderately high heat. When almost boiling, tip in the flour and sugar and beat hard until the mixture forms a ball. Beat in the eggs, a little at a time.
3) In a deep, heavy skillet heat about 3 inches oil to 370°F. Either fill a pastry bag with the mixture and squeeze 2-inch lengths or drop teaspoonfuls of dough into the oil.
4) As the churros rise and brown, lift out, drain on paper towels and dust with the sugar/cinnamon mixture. Serve.

Cilicote en Almibar

Serves 4–6

Cilicote are also known as Golden Apples, but this is somewhat of a misnomer as they are actually more like plums. They have a fabulous sweet sour taste and are beautifully fragrant. If they prove impossible to find, use apricots in this light compote.

1 lb (approx. 3–4 cups) Golden
   Apples (see above)
¾ cup superfine sugar
¾ cup water
1 vanilla bean, slit open

1 clove
a small stick of cinnamon
a long strip of lime peel

1) Put everything in a pan with a tight-fitting lid. Bring slowly to a boil and simmer for 10 minutes. Serve warm or well chilled.

Cook's Note

If desired, remove the warm Golden Apples and place on a glass dish. Reduce the syrup until very thick and dribble over the fruit.

Flan with Mexican Fruit Salad

Serves 4–6

Flan is very popular in Mexico. We are perhaps more familiar with it as crème caramel. Instant mixes and ready-mades are available in most supermarkets. If you have more time, make your own: it doesn't take long to prepare but requires slow cooking, which puts it outside the scope of this book.

4 tablespoons superfine sugar

finely grated rind and juice of a lime

½ cup water

2 guavas, peeled and cubed

1 large avocado, peeled and cubed

1 grenadillo or 2 small passion fruits

1 small pineapple, peeled and cubed

2 pitahaya (cactus fruit), peeled and cubed

1 large ripe mango, peeled and cubed

6 individual crème caramels

2 tablespoons toasted flaked almonds

2 tablespoons toasted flaked coconut

1) In a saucepan dissolve the sugar in the lime juice and water over low heat. Bring to a boil. Add the guavas.

2) Simmer for 5 minutes then add the rest of the fruits, scraping in the contents of the grenadillo or passion fruit, and the lime zest. Chill.

3) To serve, unmold the crème caramels. Surround with the fruit salad and scatter over the flaked almonds and coconut.

Helado de Coco

Serves 4—6

You will need a sorbetière or ice-cream maker for this quick coconut ice cream. Although you need to make sure you freeze the bowl for at least 24 hours beforehand, the actual "working" time in this recipe is very short.

Do use the rum as the alcohol prevents the ice from freezing too hard.

14 fl oz can coconut milk,
  shaken

6 tablespoons corn syrup
  mixed together with 6 tablespoons hot water

1 cup plus 3 tablespoons half-
  and-half

2 tablespoons rum

1) In a bowl beat everything together with a large whisk and pour into the ice-cream maker as the paddles are churning. Let the machine run until the mixture is frozen—depending on type, this is 10–25 minutes.

2) Serve or scrape into a plastic container, seal and freeze for later use.

Cook's Note

This ice cream is delicious with a drizzle of grenadine or lime syrup.

Leche Quemada

Serves 4–6

This is a very sweet, rich pudding. Unless you have a very sweet tooth, I suggest you use the fudgey caramel as a filling or topping. Personally, I prefer it over ice cream or on a steamed pudding or plain sponge cake.

Authentically, this dish takes hours to prepare—time is slashed in this recipe by using evaporated milk. The result is opaque and a little thicker. Another option for a similar milk caramel is the old boarding school treat of boiling a can of condensed milk, but this takes rather longer than 30 minutes.

Alice B. Toklas recounts the mysterious Señora B.'s recipe for *Dulce* in her cookbook and then gives her own, adding somewhat sniffily "There are people who like it a lot."

4 fl oz. can evaporated milk	a pinch of baking soda
1 cup light brown sugar	2 tablespoons rum

1) In a saucepan melt the sugar slowly in the milk over low heat, stirring to dissolve. When you can no longer hear grittiness, add the baking soda and bring the milk to a boil. Cook, stirring, while the mixture darkens and thickens. Beat in the rum and serve.

Cook's Note

Nuts—pecans, almonds and walnuts—or coconut can be added. This caramel is also delicious over fresh sliced pears, hulled strawberries and halved peaches.

Lime and Almond Clusters

Serves 4–6

Known simply as *dulce*—sweets (candies)—these are often made for Mexico's big celebration for the Day of the Dead. Looked at from afar, the preparations for the festivities seem gruesome or morbid. Children are given sugar skulls or coffins with their names piped on them. Elaborate cakes and sweetmeats are taken to the graves of dead relatives. However, in a country where many families are touched by early death, it is a way of remembering loved ones, and it seems more relevant than the commercialized festivities of Halloween.

½ cup evaporated milk	juice and rind of a lime
1½ cups sugar	½ cup flaked almonds

1) In a saucepan heat the milk with 1 cup of the sugar over moderate heat until heated through.

2) In a separate pan, melt the remaining ½ cup sugar over low heat, stirring occasionally. As it begins to caramelize, slowly add the juice of the lime. Add the sweetened milk. Boil to 234°F—the soft ball stage on a candy thermometer.

3) Beat in the almonds and then drop spoonfuls on a greased baking sheet to cool.

Nieve

Serves 6

Nieve brings back simple childhood memories—*Mr. Frostie,* a toy for making shaved ice, will come back into his own here. Those unlucky enough never to have made his acquaintance will have to make do with a heavy-duty blender.

6 cups of shaved ice   a few mint leaves
6 tablespoons grenadine syrup

1)   Divide the ice between 6 sundae glasses, pour over the syrup and top with the mint leaves. Easy!

Cook's Note

Other liqueurs or fruit syrups can be used. *Kahlua* (coffee), *Curaçao* (orange), concentrated apple juice or lemon or lime syrup are especially good.

Nuez con Caramelo

Serves 4–6

Mexicans have a rather sweet tooth. This version of nut brittle with pecans is found all over. Others, made with peanuts, walnuts (nuez de Castilla) and seeds, also exist.

1 cup light brown sugar   1 cup shelled pecans

1) In a heavy-bottomed pan, melt the sugar slowly, stirring constantly. When it caramelizes (the "crack stage"—310°F on a candy thermometer), stir in the pecans.

2) Spread out onto a lightly oiled baking sheet, cool and then break into pieces.

Sweet Chimichangas

Serves 4–6

2 tablespoons light brown
  sugar
2 teaspoons ground cinnamon
3 large ripe bananas, halved
  lengthwise

6 flour tortillas
1 orange or lime
oil or butter for frying
crème fraîche

1) In a small bowl mix together the brown sugar and cinnamon.
2) Dust the banana halves with the mixture.
3) Place one half on each tortilla. Squeeze over a little juice from the orange or lime.
4) Fold up the bottom of the tortilla over the banana. Fold in the sides, roll up and secure with a toothpick.
5) In a skillet cook the tortillas in the oil or butter over moderate heat until golden and serve immediately with some crème fraîche.

Sweet Fried Bananas

Serves 4–6

This gooey sweet mess is delicious on its own or used as a topping for store-bought or homemade ice cream. Alternatively, serve as a cheesecake topping or with an egg custard—set or pouring. Authentically, it would be served with thick sour cream—use crème fraîche as the best widely available substitute.

⅓ cup butter

4–5 medium bananas, sliced

½ cup flaked almonds or pecan halves

½ cup light brown sugar

2 teaspoons ground cinnamon

2 tablespoons rum or orange juice

1) In a skillet melt the butter over moderate heat and in it cook the bananas until lightly brown.

2) Add the nuts and cook another minute before adding the remaining ingredients. Stir carefully until the sugar has melted and the mixture is bubbling. Serve.

Cook's Note

Two squares of Mexican chocolate or good dark chocolate can be added to the bananas just before serving. Stir gently to melt into the mixture.

Sweet Tamales

Serves 4–6

*I*f you don't have any coconut milk, use dairy milk or even pineapple juice instead. In the summer months try adding wild strawberries, currants or blueberries in place of the candied fruit.

1 cup instant polenta
¾ cup coconut milk
½ cup water
2 tablespoons light brown
   sugar

2 tablespoons candied fruit—
   pineapple, mango, papaya—
   chopped or 2 tablespoons
   raisins

1) In a skillet cook all ingredients over moderate heat until the mixture leaves the sides cleanly.
2) Shape into cigars and roll loosely in wax paper, twisting the ends. Place in a steamer over boiling water for 20 minutes and serve.

Cook's Note

After steaming, the sweet tamales can be cooked in butter and dusted with a mixture of ground cinnamon and confectioners' sugar.

"Tuna Salad"

Serves 4–6

There's nothing fishy about this. Tuna is the Mexican name for cactus fruit or prickly pears. You may also see them sold as barbary figs. Take care when handling them as they are prickly! Small sharp hairs stick out of little knobs on the yellowy skin, so wear gloves. If you cannot find prickly pears, the similar pitahaya can be substituted instead—they don't bite, but the flavor is blander.

2 tablespoons superfine sugar	6 prickly pears
1 teaspoon ground ginger	½ a lime

1) In a small bowl combine the sugar and ginger.
2) Cut a thin slice from the top and bottom of the prickly pears and then slit the skin lengthways, but not too deeply. Peel away the skin and take out the flesh. Sometimes it is a vivid pinky purple and at others an apricot yellow. Cut into chunks and place on a glass plate.
3) Squeeze over the lime and sprinkle with the sugar and ginger. Leave in a cool place until serving.

Zapote

Serves 4–6

The names of this hard leathery-skinned plum-sized fruit are a bit mixed up—you might also find sapote or sapodilla. Whatever their name, wait until they are rather squishy (their names apparently derive from the Aztec "tzapotl" meaning soft). The under-ripe fruit is white inside; when ready it turns a custardy yellow. You can use them for milk-shakes too.

4 cups zapote	1 teaspoon zest of orange,
superfine sugar to taste	lemon or lime

1) Halve the fruit, throw away the central pits, and scoop out the middles and place in a serving bowl.
2) Mash with a fork, adding sugar to taste. Serve garnished with the citrus zest.

Cook's Note

You can serve these more simply—just scoop with a small teaspoon like you would an avocado.

Drinks

Agua de Jamaica

Serves 4–6

Indistinguishable from the Egyptian *Karkade,* this beautiful ruby-colored drink can be served hot or cold. The dried flowers are from the hibiscus and can be found in most natural food shops and some supermarkets. They are even available in tea bags!

1 cup hibiscus flowers	sugar to taste
4 cups water	cinnamon sticks, 1 per glass

1) In a saucepan or tea kettle bring the hibiscus flowers and water to a boil.
2) Leave in a warm place to steep for 20 minutes.
3) Strain through a paper coffee filter and sweeten to taste.
4) Serve with a cinnamon stick in each glass. To serve cold, chill well.

Café de Olla

Serves 4–6

❧✤❧

Coffee in the Middle East is very similar to this Mexican version: simply exchange carda-mom for the cinnamon. This is an intensely flavored, very warming brew, ideal for those of us who live in chillier climes.

2 cups water
2 cinnamon sticks
1–2 cloves
4 tablespoons freshly ground
   coffee—use a superfine grind

3–6 tablespoons brown sugar
   (to taste—with 6 it is almost
   syrupy)

1) Combine everything in a coffee pot or saucepan. Heat until just simmering, stirring occasionally. Keep warm. Strain and serve.

Horchata

Serves 4–6

Horchata in Mexico varies enormously. Sometimes it is made with rice, sometimes with melon seeds or almonds. The main ingredient in this horchata is tiger nuts—the original Spanish ingredient. These are not really nuts at all but rather shriveled-looking tubers. They are also known as *chufas* in Spain or "earth almonds." A bag of tiger nuts will keep you quiet for hours as they are quite chewy and are like munching fresh coconut—even though your jaws ache, you can't quite stop!

This is an altogether more civilized way of consuming them, especially if you add a shot of *Kahlua* (Mexican coffee liqueur) to the horchata first.

1 cup tiger nuts (available in natural foods stores)	2½ cups cold water sugar to taste (optional)

1) Grind the nuts in a heavy-duty blender or food processor with a little of the water. Add the remaining water and process briefly.
2) Strain into a pitcher and serve cold, adding sugar to taste, if desired.

Cook's Note

It is not unusual for lime to be added to the horchata or, as described above, *Kahlua* can be added or a little cinnamon.

Hot Chocolate

Serves 4–6

꧁꧂

*B*anish winter blues with a steaming mug of this—it beats any commercially available powdered drink and really doesn't take much longer to make. If you can find Mexican chocolate, you can omit the almond and cinnamon. Use milk or water or half-and-half.

3 cups milk (or see above)   ½ cup dark chocolate, grated
2 tablespoons ground almonds   1 teaspoon ground cinnamon
1 stick cinnamon

1) In a saucepan heat the milk with the almond and cinnamon over low heat. Keep hot for 5 minutes, allowing the flavors to infuse.
2) Strain onto the chocolate in a warm jug and whisk until the chocolate has melted into the milk.
3) Pour into individual mugs and serve with a sprinkle of cinnamon.

Licuado de Agua

Serves 4–6

Instead of a milky fruit shake, this one's made with water and fruit. It can also be made with sparkling water. Instead of using sugar, you could try adding a fruit syrup, such as grenadine, to add color, flavor and sweetness. Substitute whichever fruit you have on hand—peaches, nectarines and papaya all make great drinks.

1 medium pineapple, peeled,
    cored and cut into chunks
4 cups ice-cold water
sugar to taste—depends on the
    sweetness of the fruit

mint sprigs
lime slices

1) Process the pineapple and water in a blender.
2) Strain into a pitcher and sweeten. Float the mint and lime on the top.

sangritas

Serves 4

Tomato juice never tasted like this before. Use this non-alcoholic drink as a starter or aperitif. You can, if desired, add tequila to taste.

juice of 3 limes

salt

1–2 small red pequín or birds-
eye chilies, crushed and
chopped

1½ cups tomato juice

½ cup freshly squeezed orange
juice

2–3 tablespoons grenadine
syrup

1) Dip or brush the rims of 4 glasses in or with the lime juice then dip in the salt. Chill well.
2) In a pitcher combine the remaining lime juice with a pinch of salt.
3) Add the rest of the ingredients.
4) Leave in a cold place until serving then strain into the prepared glasses.

Margaritas

Serves 6

*T*here seem to be as many ways to make a Margarita, that archetypal Mexican cocktail, as there are to make the perfect martini. Here is just one.

1 cup tequila	ice
½ cup Cointreau or other orange liqueur	fresh strawberries or peaches, sliced
½ cup lime juice	6 sprigs of mint

1) In a pitcher mix the liquids together.
2) Divide the ice between 6 chilled glasses. (See the Sangritas recipe on page 135 for how to salt the rims.)
3) Add fruit to the glasses and pour over the tequila mixture. Top each with a sprig of mint.

Mexican Chocolate II

Serves 4–6

◆

*T*his is a grown-up, sophisticated version of hot chocolate. It is very rich and smooth — it can be served instead of or after dessert.

⅓ cup Mexican or dark
    chocolate, grated
1 teaspoon ground cinnamon
2–4 tablespoons sugar
½ cup boiling water

½ cup hot milk
½ cup hot strong coffee
a little orange rind
1 tablespoon sherry

1) In a bowl over barely simmering water, melt the chocolate with the cinnamon and sugar. When melted, whisk in the boiling water. Stir frequently for 2 minutes, then whisk in the milk, coffee, orange rind and sherry. Pour into small cups and serve.

Mexican Strawberry Milkshakes

Serves 6

*O*ne that kids of every age will really enjoy—in Spanish it is *licuado de leche*.

4 cups cold milk
3¼ cups small ripe strawberries, hulled

4 tablespoons superfine
   sugar—add more to taste
6 sprigs of mint

1) In the blender mix all of the ingredients until smooth. Strain and serve with a sprig of mint on each tall glass.

Té

Serves 4–6

Tea in Mexico normally means an herb tea. The two most common are *Manzanillo* (chamomile) or *Yerbabuena* (mint). The method is the same in both cases. The teas are usually served at the end of the meal as a digestif, much like Pedro Conejo (Peter Rabbit) was dosed after overeating in Mr. MacGregor's vegetable patch!

> 1 oz. dried chamomile flowers or mint leaves
>
> 2 cups boiling water
> sugar to taste

1) Put the chamomile or mint into a clean teapot. Pour on the boiling water and leave to infuse for 5 minutes. Strain into cups and sweeten to taste.

Cook's Note

Herbal teas are available in bags—however, check for additives, many now come with extra flavorings. A straightforward tea is required for authenticity.

Index